THE
DRINKING MAN'S
SURVIVAL GUIDE

Nic van Oudtshoorn

Take That Books

THE DRINKING MAN'S SURVIVAL GUIDE

Take That Books is an imprint of
Take That Ltd.
PO Box 200
Harrogate
HG1 4XB

Published by arrangement with
MaxiBooks, PO Box 529, Kiama, NSW 2533, Australia

Disclaimer

Cartoons:
SHANE SUMMERTON & JACKSON GRAHAM.

Cover Design:
LOOK SERIOUS DESIGN, Sydney, Australia. Tel: (02) 560-9464
Cover illustration: Barry Rickwood.

Contents

Drinker's IQ Test

Become a Doctor of Drinking Science

REMEMBER the bloke whose wife accompanied him to his favourite watering hole to find out what the great attraction was that kept him there for hours on end? He ordered his usual whisky. She asked for the same. The drinks came, she took a sip, pulled an awful face and cried out: "This stuff tastes vile!" Her husband tossed back his drink, tried his best to look pained, then replied: "And you're always saying I come here to enjoy myself!"

To wives and wowsers, drinking is a strange way, indeed, to get pleasure. And let's face it, the first few times we all took a drink, it did taste pretty awful. It's by persevering that one learns (often, thankfully, only too quickly) to experience the joys that turn you into a confirmed and happy Drinking Man.

Even if you never learn to like the taste of booze (and that's a very remote possibility, indeed), don't despair. Some of the world's greatest drinking men have had the same problem — but that never prevented them from enjoying the rewards of drinking. Take the famous American writer Jack London, who explained his unusual dilemma in his book *John Barleycorn*:

"This physical loathing for alcohol I have never got over. But I have conquered it. To this day I conquer it every time I take a drink. The palate never ceases to rebel, and the palate can be trusted to know what is good for the body. But men do not drink for the effect alcohol produces on the body. What they drink for is the brain effect; and if it must come through the body, so much the worse for the body."

As London found, there's no pleasure without pain. To qualify as a Drinking Man, you must be prepared for some hard work: you'll have to learn a great deal about booze and boozing, and swallow hundreds, perhaps even thousands, of drinks as part of the rigorous training. This kind of knowledge doesn't come cheap, either — you'll be called on to invest a fair bit of time and money to learn the finer pleasures of drinking.

But the rewards are far greater than you can ever imagine. It's a course of study that never ends — and when you're off to the pub, you can always tell the wife (and any wowsers who dare to enquire): "I have to attend my course!"

Better still, you can prove that you've not been lying by qualifying as a DOCTOR OF DRINKING SCIENCE! It's easy — as soon as you've laughed your way through this book with a drink or ten in hand (and passed the Drinker's

IQ Test), simply send stamps to the value of £1.50 to cover postage and packing to the address on page 192. In return we'll send you a 'degree certificate', printed on quality marbled paper, to hang up in your home bar. Don't forget to tell us the name you want on the certificate.

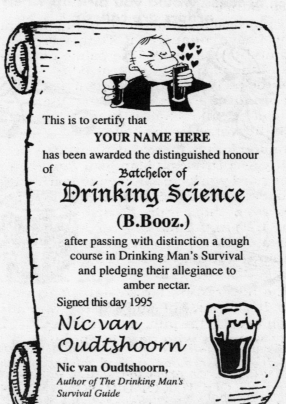

This is to certify that

YOUR NAME HERE

has been awarded the distinguished honour of

Batchelor of

Drinking Science

(B.Booz.)

after passing with distinction a tough course in Drinking Man's Survival and pledging their allegiance to amber nectar.

Signed this day 1995

Nic van Oudtshoorn

Nic van Oudtshoorn,
Author of The Drinking Man's Survival Guide

Drinker's  I.Q. Test

No.1: TAKE YOUR PICK

Which of these would you pick up when last orders are called?

A  **B**

C  **D**

Answers on Page 189

A man went to the doctor with a storming headache and nausea. The doctor made a thorough examination and proclaimed that he couldn't find anything wrong.

Smelling alcohol on the man's breath the doctor offered the explanation, "It must be the heavy drinking." "That's OK," said the man, "I'll come back when you are sober."

Drinking is good for you

IN HIS aptly titled book, *Whisky*, James Ross recounts the true story of Robert Warner who, in 1840, was charged an extra premium when he applied for life insurance — because he did not drink! The company's doctors insisted total abstainers had a shorter lifespan than drinkers — a common medical opinion at the time.

There can be no argument that drinking, in moderation, is good for you. Take Noah, that great survivor of the Flood and, according to the Bible, the first man to plant a vine and make wine after the earth had dried out.

He also became the first drunk and the first flasher, but those are incidentals. What is important is that after tasting the fruit of the vine he lived for another *three hundred and fifty years*! In more modern times, a fisherman named Harry Jenkins lived to the age of 165 — because, he said, he drank a gallon of strong ale every day!

To survive as a Drinking Man, you'll probably need to convince wives and wowsers alike that going to the

! SCOTTISH NECTAR !

THE CELEBRATED

UAM-VAR WHISKY.

ELEVEN AWARDS

TIDSWELL, WILSON & Cᵒ

60 CLARENCE, Sᵗ SYDNEY.

AGENTS IN NEW SOUTH WALES.

· TRIUMPH · OF THE GOOD SPIRIT OVER BAD.

pub is like going to a health farm or a doctor. It's a duty you owe to your body and to your family who depend on you, because being healthy will also make you wealthy and wise.

However, be prepared for a lot of scepticism when you first raise this argument — no matter how true it is. But don't be daunted: the rest of this chapter is packed with proof (religious, medical, literary and plain common sense) which you can use with devastating effect to convince the doubters.

It says so in the Bible

The Bible has mainly good things to say about drinking of alcohol, which it mentions 165 times in both the Old and the New Testament. Here are a few

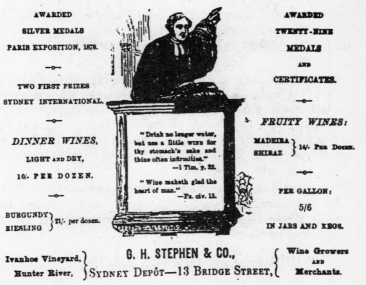

examples you can quote with glee (as Australian advertisers, like the one above, did around the turn of the century):

Wine measurably drunk and in season bringeth gladness of the heart, and cheerfulness of the mind...

— ECCLESIASTES 34:29-30

There is a crying for wine in the streets, the lack of which takes all joy of life away.

— ISAIAH 24:11

In the New Testament, Jesus' first miracle was to make wine so wedding guests could have a good time.

He also served wine at the Last Supper. St Paul, too, advised early Christians: *"Drink no longer water, but use a little wine for thy stomach's sake and thine often impurities."*

Most of the world's other great religions, from the earliest times, advocated the use of alcoholic refreshments, not only to improve the health of the body, but even as a way of having communion with the gods. As part of their prayers, ancient Hebrews used to bless and thank God for having created the fruit of the vine.

The medieval Christian church certainly believed in the goodness of beer and ale, with more than 400,000 litres served at the enthronement of one archbishop of York.

Ask the doctor

Modern-day medical science has raised many excellent arguments in favour of drinking, as some of the very latest research findings show:

✔ *Two schooners of beer a day reduces the risk of gall bladder trouble, diabetes, heart attacks and strokes for men, according to Simon de Burgh of Sydney University's Public Health Department.*

✔ *Red wine "significantly" lowers the amount of potentially harmful cholesterol in the blood, French cardiology researchers announced in 1990.*

✔ *"Light or moderate consumption of alcohol reduces the risk of coronary disease," according to Sir Richard Doll, one of the world's leading epidemiologists.*

Throughout history, many doctors have turned to wine and other alcoholic drinks as a way to cure many

kinds of ailments. One 18th century diary records how a young girl who suffered "a bad knee" was ordered by the doctor to drink "at least a pint of port wine a day". She recovered.

Often, doctors take their own (alcoholic) medicine — and thrive as a result.

A prime example is Harvard University's first medical graduate, who lived to the age of 100. When celebrating his centenary, Dr Augustus Holyoke attributed his longevity and good health to drinking two litres of cider mixed with rum daily — with breakfast, lunch and dinner.

When Marian Taggart was born in Britain in 1938, she was only 31cm (12in) long and weighed a mere 283gm (10 oz), which according to the *Guinness Book of Records* is the lowest birth weight ever recorded for a surviving infant, of which there is definite evidence.

TEMPERANCE THERMOMETER

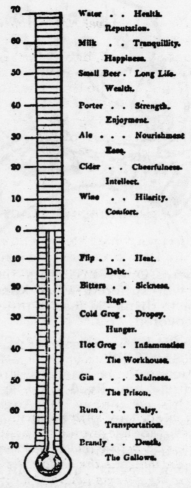

70	Water . . Health.	
	Reputation.	
60	Milk . . Tranquillity.	
	Happiness.	
50	Small Beer . Long Life.	
	Wealth.	
40	Porter . . Strength.	
	Enjoyment.	
30	Ale . . . Nourishment	
	Ease.	
20	Cider . . Cheerfulness.	
	Intellect.	
10	Wine . . Hilarity.	
	Comfort.	
0		
10	Flip . . . Heat.	
	Debt.	
20	Bitters . . Sickness.	
	Rags.	
30	Cold Grog . Dropsy.	
	Hunger.	
40	Hot Grog . Inflammation	
	The Workhouse.	
50	Gin . . . Madness.	
	The Prison.	
60	Rum . . . Palsy.	
	Transportation.	
70	Brandy . . Death.	
	The Gallows.	

Wowser's propaganda ... This 19th century "Temperance Thermometer" quite wrongly rates water tops and brandy last in terms of goodness for the user. For a true reading, turn it upside down.

And how did she survive? Not by taking mother's milk, but thanks to brandy!

For the first 30 hours, baby Marian was fed hourly with brandy, glucose and water through a fountain-pen filler. By the time she turned 21, Marian weighed a healthy 48kg (7st 8lb).

In fact, the health-giving qualities of booze even for babies was known as far back as the 15th century, when wet nurses were forbidden by law to drink water. To produce the purest milk, it was stipulated that "her beverage must be a pure wine".

As Shakespeare said...

Every educated person quotes the Bard with approval, so why not the Drinking Man in honour and defence of drink? The great playwright greatly approved of drinking, both for it's health-giving properties and because it gives the drinker "excellent wit". As he put it so eloquently in *Henry IV Part 2*

> *If I had a thousand sons, the first humane principle I would teach them, should be to forswear thin potations, and to addict themselves to sack [sherry].*

Elsewhere in the same play, the wonderful properties of liquor are shown to include *"the warming of the blood: which before (cold, and settled) left the liver white, and pale; which is the badge of pusillanimity, and cowardice: but the sherris [sherry] warms it, and makes it course from the inwards..."*

Other poets, writers and philosophers, too, have long known the benefits for body and soul of drinking a dram or a draught (or both):

> *Let schoolmasters puzzle their brain,*
> *With grammar, and nonsense, and learning,*
> *Good Liquor, I stoutly maintain,*
> *Gives genius a better discerning.*

> — OLIVER GOLDSMITH
> *SHE STOOPS TO CONQUER.*

Charles Dickens' advice for curing a cold (as recorded in his novel *Hard Times*): "Take a glass of scalding rum-and-butter after you get into bed."

And this is how the 16th century Irish writer Staynhurst described the many beneficent qualities of Irish whiskey: "Being moderately taken, it sloweth age, it strengtheneth youth, it helpeth digestion, it cutteth flegme, it abandoneth melancholie, it relisheth the heart, it quickeneth the mind, it lighteneth the spirit. And trulie it is a soveraigne liquor."

> *"Wine moistens the soul and lulls our grief*
> *to sleep, while it also awakens kindly*
> *feelings."*

> — SOCRATES.

And from that great writer Anonymous (he appears often in this book) comes the following true words:

> *The horse and mule live 30 years*
> *And nothing know of wine and beers.*
> *The goat and sheep at 20 die*
> *And never taste of Scotch or Rye.*
> *The cow drinks water by the ton*
> *And at 18 is mostly done.*
> *The dog at 15 cashes in*

Without the aid of rum and gin...
All animals are strictly dry:
They sinless live and swiftly die;
But sinful, ginful, rum-soaked men
Survive for three score years and ten.
And some of them, a very few,
Stay pickled till they're 92.

Wisdom of the ages

Call them old wives' recipes or the wisdom of our ancestors, there's no doubt many old cures relied on booze to treat everything from the common cold to smallpox — and most ailments in between! Here are two for the common cold:

☆ Drinking hot wine curdled with wine or spiced ale, a concoction known as "posset", was a favourite in Elizabethan England.

☆ An old Scots remedy recommends you "take your toddy to bed, put one bowler hat at the foot, and drink until you see two".

Schoolboys were allowed a regular allowance of beer in ancient Egypt, because local doctors said it helped them grow strong. Girls, it appears, did not enjoy the same privilege, because they were not meant to be warriors.

A true cock-and-ale tale

Cock ale was sold at taverns called *The Cock* a couple of centuries ago — and was claimed to cure everything from whooping cough to colic, consumption, dropsy, worms and "the bloody flux".

Cock ale was the most popular and health-giving kind of "Beer Cup" — others had names like Humpty-dumpty, Clamber-clown, Hugmatee, Stick-back, and Knock-me-down. If you want to sample Cock Ale, in it's day famed as a "very strengthening and restorative compound", here's the recipe:

Take a cock of half a year old, kill him and truss him well, and put into a cash twelve gallons of Ale to which add four pounds of raisins of the sun, well picked, stoned, washed and dryed; sliced Dates, half a pound; nutmegs and mace two ounces: Infuse the dates and spices in a quart of canary twenty-four hours, then boil the cock in a manner to a jelly, till a gallon of water is reduced to two quarts; then press the body of him extremely well, and put the liquor into the cask where the Ale is, with the spices and fruit, adding a few blades of mace; then put to it a pint of new Ale yeast, and let it work well for a day, and, in two days, you may broach it for use or, in hot weather, the second day; and if it proves too strong, you may add more plain Ale to palliate this restorative drink, which contributes much to the invigorating of nature.

These Beer Cup concoctions were served into small glasses from containers called posset pots: delicate glass bowls with one or two handles.

Drinking Man's Hall of Fame

AFTER almost 3000 arrests for being drunk and disorderly in a public place, 66-year-old Tommy Johns died in Brisbane in 1988 — but not, as you might suspect, from alcoholism. It was a brain tumour that ended a drinking career which won the courageous Aussie tippler a place in the *Guinness Book of Records*.

If you feel like yelling "Geronimo" when you've had a few, you're in very good company. Indian chief Geronimo loved his tequila so much that he invariably rode into battle with a bottle or so of this firewater inside him. His unusual brand of "Dutch courage" won him a place in history.

Chided about being tipsy, Buffalo Bill Cody once took an oath to drink only one glass of whiskey a day. When he came to his senses, he quickly acquired a glass holding almost two litres of the frontier firewater — so he could drink as before without breaking his word.

Former world heavyweight boxing champion John L. Sullivan could absorb bare-knuckle punches and booze with equal dexterity. His record at the bar? Sixty-seven gin fizzes — before walking out by himself!

"I MAY NOT FRIGHTEN YOU, BUT MY BOOZE BREATH WILL KNOCK YOU OUT!"

Britain's 18th century prime minister William Pitt the Younger coped with the affairs of state by having a drink or two. But one year, when the Australian convict colony was particularly troublesome, the man after whom Sydney's Pitt Street was named, outdid himself by quaffing 574 bottles of claret, 854 bottles of Madeira and 2,410 bottles of port!

Author Dylan Thomas enjoyed nothing more than kippers for breakfast — but only if he could wash them down with a pint or two of Guinness.

Charlie Smith, who at the age of 137 fielded the inevitable questions from journalists about what caused his longevity, replied: "Lots of vitamins every day — washed down with rum!"

The Duke of Monmouth was so fond of rum that on the way to the scaffold, he called out for a cup of "hot rum and eggs". He gulped it down just before his head left his body.

How's this for heaven: a place where you are rushed to the pearly gates by nubile angels with gigantic containers of beer and where a magic goat produces huge quantities of beer instead of milk!

If you think that's worth dying for, you're on the same wavelength as pagan Germanic warriors, who believed that those slain in battle were transported to Valhalla ("Hall of the Slain") by divine maidens called Valkyries who carried huge horns filled to the brim with foaming beer.

A wonderful feature of Valhalla was the goat Heidrun, whose teats produced huge quantities of

"WE'VE RUN OUT OF WATER! THIS IS A CRISIS, HODGES — WHAT AM I GOING TO PUT IN MY WHISKY?"

beer every day, enough to keep the warriors permanently intoxicated. Heidrun was a popular name for earthly goats belonging to wishful thinkers.

Downing 80 litres of beer during the course of one evening is a stupendous feat at any time — and was enough to win a medieval baron named Gambrinus the position he still holds as Flemish patron saint of beer.

Drink researcher Richard Erdoes, in his book *1000 Amazing Facts about Booze*, records a turn-of-the-century Bavarian as drinking 150 glasses of beer every day, and a German-American of Cincinnati who downed 188 glasses of beer between sunrise and sunset during one hot summer day to win a bet.

If you speak English and you like a drink or three, blame your forefathers. Saxons (the non-Angelic part of our make-up) only stopped drinking when they passed out or were to sick to continue, according to 12th century historian William of Malmesbury. He added: "They [the Saxons] think they have not treated their guests well if they are not so full of drink that they vomit."

Royalty continued that great drinking tradition. Queen Elizabeth I had two large bumpers of beer as an eye-opener every morning, while Queen Victoria loved to drink half a tumbler of red wine, topped up with Scotch whisky. She was naturally strongly opposed to teetotalism — so much so that she refused to promote one Anglican minister to the position of Dean until he agreed to stop promoting total abstinence.

Having a blood-alcohol reading of over 0.05mg per 100ml of blood is enough to land a driver in jail in many parts of the world, because legally you are considered too drunk to control a motor vehicle. So imagine the state a 24-year old female was in when she was admitted to the California University Medical School in Los Angeles in 1982 with a reading of 1.51mg per 100ml. Reported to be "confused but conscious" when admitted, she discharged herself after two days — and reportedly headed for the nearest pub for a top-up!

Beer certainly is healthy for you, but it can lead to a slight weight gain, as William Lewis discovered before his death in 1793. His obituary tells how Thirsty Willie made it a rule, every morning of his life, to read a number of chapters in the Bible — and in the evening to drink eight gallons of ale.

Sadly, one evening he was running short of ale, so he topped up his intake with wine — which gave him such colic that he died.

"It is calculated," says one contemporary report, "that in his lifetime he must have drunk a sufficient quantity to float a seventy-four gun warship. His size was astonishing, and he averaged 40 stone. Although he died in his parlour, it was found necessary to construct a machine in the form of a crane, to lift his body in a carriage, and afterwards to have the machine

to let him down into the grave."

Whether Willie left a bequest to buy the mourners a pint or two is not recorded.

A few centuries ago, ardent drinkers seemed to consume far greater quantities of alcohol than is the norm today — better still, this was accepted as quite normal.

For almost a quarter of a century, a popular Lord Mayor of London washed down his breakfast with 5 litres of strong ale.

Roman emperor Maximin's greatest claim to fame was that he could pour 30 litres of wine down his throat during dinner.

That's more of a feat than you may think — because Romans' favoured their wines "flavoured" with a combination of sea-water, turpentine, rosin and pitch!

Drinker's I.Q. Test

No.2: MATCH THE DRINKS

BELOW are 15 popular spirits. In the glass next to each bottle, insert the number from the list at the bottom of the page which shows the main ingredients used in its manufacture. Some drinks shown use the same basic ingredients, while at least one of the ingredients listed is not used to make any of the drinks shown.

Cognac | Armanac | Aquavlt

Bourbon | Silvowltz | Vodka

Curacao | Irish Whlskey | Scotch

Sake | Schnapps | Rum

Tequlla | Calvados | Arak

1. Cherries
2. Oranges
3. Plums
4. Barley (malted and unmalted), wheat, rye and oats
5. Potatoes
6. Grapes
7. Molasses
8. Rye, corn and barley malt
9. Apples
10. Rice
11. Barley
12. Wormwood
13. Juice of the Century plant
14. Juniper berries.
15. Wheat

Answers on Page 189

Drink, drink — and be merry!

GETTING drunk is the price we all have to pay at some time or other for the enjoyment of drinking ... and it's an experience unlike any other. You find yourself becoming witty and convivial, a brilliant speaker blessed with rapier-sharp repartee, a fearless opponent of injustice and your employer alike, a generous host, a man about town. The world suddenly looks much brighter, the women so much more beautiful with every drink you consume ...

Centuries ago, the Earl of Rochester put it this way: *"Oh, that second bottle, it is the sincerest, wisest, and the most impartial downright friend we have; tells the truth, of ourselves, and forces us to speak truth of others; banishes flattery from our tongues and distrust from our hearts..."*

So long as you don't drive or play around with guns, getting drunk on occasion is usually quite harmless. (That is, to anyone but yourself the next morning, but more about that later. Our concern here is strictly with the joys of drinking — let the suffering wait.)

BOTTLED BEAUTY!

A torrid tale of liquid lust!

Being intoxicated has been so universal a pleasure, for such a long time, that there are more words to describe it than any other condition — in almost every language on earth! American researcher Paul Dickson once compiled 2241 synonyms for being drunk; his publisher deemed only 1224 fit for publication. Here's a sampling:

As drunk as
    a fiddler
    a lord
    a piper
    a tinker
    David's sow
    a beggar
    a pig
as happy as a
    king
as merry as a grig
afflicted
arseholed
balmy
been in the sun
beery
blind drunk
blotto
boiled
bombed
boozed
boozy
bosky
bottled
breezy

buffy
canned
cast away
caught it
chases geese
chateau'd
chocfull
cock-eyed
cocksy-boozy
concerned
corned
crocked
cup-sprung
cut
dagged
disguised
doped up
elevated
far-gone
floppy
flushed
flustered
foggy
foxed
fresh

fuddled
fuddled
full
full-cocked
funny
gilded
ginned up
glassy-eyed
gone
got
    a dish
    a skinful
    his load
gravy-eyed
groggy
half-cocked
half-seas over
happy
has copped the
    brewer
has had a drop
    too much
has had one over
    the eight
hazy

high
in a quandary
in drink
in his cups
in liquor
inebriated
inked
intoxicated
jagged
juiced
legless
lit up
loaded
looped
loppy
lumpy
lushy
maudlin
mellow
messed up
miraculous
mops and brooms
muddled
muggy
muzzy

nailed it	plastered	soaked	tiddly
nappy	ploughed	soused	tight
nicely thank you	polluted	sozzled	tipsy
not able to see a	raddled	springy	top-heavy
hole through	ripe	squiffy	turned-on
a ladder	ripped	stiff	under the
obfuscated	screwed	stinking drunk	influence
oiled	sees double	stinko	the table
out	sewed-up	stinks	the weather
overcome	shot	stoned	wasted
overtaken	shows his hobnails	stung	well-primed
pickled	slaughtered	swipy	winged
pie-eyed	slewed	tanked-up	wired
pious	sloshed	three sheets to	woozy
pissed	smashed	the wind	worse for wear.

The silly saga of David's sow

Some of the above expressions have unusual, and often very funny, origins. Take the case of "as drunk as David's sow", which according to a contemporary account, originated this way in the early 18th century:

David Lloyd, a Welshman, kept an alehouse in the town of Hereford, and had a kind of monstrous sow, with six legs, which he showed to customers as a valuable rarity. This David's wife would often make herself quite drunk, and then lie down to sleep an hour or two, that she might qualify herself for the performance of her business.

But one day the house was full, and she could find no other place to sleep in but the hogsty, where her husband kept the sow above-named on clean straw; so she very orderly went in, and fell asleep by her harmonious

companion. But the sow no sooner found the door upon the jar, but out she slipt, and rambled to a considerable distance from the yard, in joy for her deliverance.

David had that day some relations come to see him, who had been against his marrying; and, to give them an opinion of his prudent choice, he took occasion to inform them he was sorry his wife was then abroad, because he would have had them see her: "For," says David, "surely man was never better matched, or met with a more quiet, sober wife than I am blest in."

They congratulated his good fortune, and were after a short time desired by David to go and see the greatest wonder of a sow that had ever been heard of in the world. He led them to his hogsty door, and opening it to its full wideness, the first thing they saw was his good wife in such a posture and condition, as, upon her starting up and calling David husband, gave occasion for a hearty fit of laughter!"

Drunk as a fiddler refers to the custom at wakes, fairs and on board ship, to reward the fiddler making music for dancing not with cash, but with liquor. When the fiddler passed out, the dance ended.

Drunk as a lord originated in the wild drinking bouts of the nobility, particularly in the 18th and 19th centuries, when men of wealth and stature considered it a point of honour to drink one another under the table.

But, near the beginning of this century, those heady days were already ending, with author Jerome K. Jerome lamenting: "Drinking is one of those subjects

Nobility at play

with which it is [now] inadvisable to appear too well acquainted. The days are gone by when it was considered manly to go to bed intoxicated every night ... In these sadly degenerate days, an evil-smelling breath, a blotchy face, a reeling gait and a husky voice are regarded as the hall-marks on the cad rather than the gentleman."

On being drunk...

Intoxication is a condition that has inspired (and afflicted) writers, artists, philosophers, poets — and almost everyone else — over the ages.

"Oh, wondrous craft!" exclaimed Pliny the Elder. "In some way or other it has been discovered that water might be made to render men drunk!"

Victor Hugo, in his great novel *Les Miserables*, refers to an ancient fable about the effects of drinking: "Upon the first goblet he read this inscription: monkey wine; upon the second: lion wine; upon the third: sheep wine; upon the fourth: swine wine. These four inscriptions expressed the four descending degrees of drunkenness: the first, that which enlivens; the second, that which irritates; the third, that which stupefies; finally the last, that which brutalises."

Aristotle posed the question: "Why is it that to the drunk everything seems to travel in a circle, and that as drunkenness gets more hold men cannot count objects at a distance? For this reason some make this a test of drunkenness. Is it because the vision is considerably distorted by the heat of the wine?"

"The ancient Goths of Germany ... had all of them a wise custom of debating every thing of importance to their state, twice," wrote Laurence Sterne in his hilarious novel *Tristram Shandy*, "that is, — once drunk, and once sober: — Drunk — that their councils might not want vigour; — and sober — that they might not want discretion."

A similar story is told of ancient Macedonia's King Philip II, father of Alexander the Great, who dearly loved his wine, as did his son. Once, when hearing a lawsuit, the King found against the woman plaintiff, who instantly declared: "I appeal!" Bemused, the king asked to whom she thought she could appeal the royal judgment. "To Philip, when sober," she replied. Next morning, the king upheld her appeal!

Drinker's I.Q. Test

No.3: LITERACY TEST

CAN YOU READ THIS

Answers on Page 189

"Will that be a schooner of fighting beer or a schooner of singing beer?"

DRUNK?
Who, me?

TO SURVIVE as a Drinking Man there is one cardinal rule you must ALWAYS adhere to:

NO MATTER HOW MUCH YOU HAVE HAD TO DRINK, YOU NEVER, EVER, ADMIT TO BEING <u>DRUNK</u>.

For you that five-letter word no longer exists. It's part of the vocabulary of wives and wowsers — a word uttered with scorn and derision by people who have never experienced the joys of drinking.

Remember, looks can be deceptive. You may look legless, sound incoherent, smell like a brewery, but you are never DRUNK. Not ever.

Of course, among Drinking Men, being drunk occasionally is no shame. You can admit your condition freely to your mates — so long as they, too, are Drinking Men.

There's an old saying that some men get drunk because they don't have a wife to go home to, while others get drunk because they do. One advantage the former group has is that there is no one at home to

complain that they:

(a) stayed in the pub for hours, and/or

(b) came home drunk/smelling like a brewery or the like.

Beware of the wife

In extreme cases, it is not unknown for a Drinking Man to get thumped on the head for arriving home under the weather.

If you're one of those unfortunate sufferers, at least be grateful you never married Mrs Percy Pearl Washington, who could put a lot of weight behind any rolling pin! Credited in the *Guinness Book of Records* as the world's heaviest woman, she tipped the scales at 399.1 kg. She was 1.83 m (6 ft) tall, wore a size 62 dress — and died in a Milwaukee hospital on 9 October 1972 from a disease known as "excessive thirst".

In most cases, however, wives (with or without rolling pins) should prove no problem for the innovative Drinking Man, the one qualified as a DOCTOR OF DRINKING SCIENCE.

Why not?

Because you simply lie/flatter/joke your way out of your (drunken) dilemma.

In doing so, however, you need to be very alert. Just remember the old truism about alcohol: *it's a liquid good for preserving almost anything except secrets.*

Master the ancient art of lying

First, prepare your lying skills by consulting the masters. You probably have a few mates who are accomplished liars — arrange to meet them in the pub for a lesson (and a drink) or two. It's an essential part of your course to qualify as a DOCTOR OF DRINKING SCIENCE.

In the unlikely event that your conscience troubles you about devoting so much drinking time to learn how to become a good liar, consider the following words of wisdom:

> *The aim of the liar is to charm, to delight, to give pleasure. He is the very basis of civilised society.*
>
> — OSCAR WILDE

> *All men are born truthful, and die liars.*
>
> — VAUNEARGUES

Ask me no questions and I'll tell you no fibs.

— OLIVER GOLDSMITH

*Lying has a kind of respect and reverence
with it. We pay the person a compliment of
acknowledging his superiority whenever we
lie to him.*

— SAMUEL BUTLER

*It is hard to believe that a man is telling the
truth when you know that you would lie if
you were in his place.*

— H.L. MENCKEN

*The most awful thing one can do is to tell the
truth. It's all right in my case, because I'm
not taken seriously.*

— GEORGE BERNARD SHAW

Next, you need to find the right mix of fact and
fiction to make your lie work. Remember Adolf
Hitler's advice in *Mein Kampf:* "In the big lie there is
always a certain force of credibility."

Or, as the Irishman said to Winston Churchill:
"There are a terrible lot of lies going around the world,
and the trouble is that half of them are true."

So make sure your lies not only sound true, but in
all probability would be true if they were not lies.

For instance, a fisherman (but not a plumber) could
get away with this one:

"I found a mermaid in my net and had to revive her
with a few drinks and then take her out to sea to the

deep fishing grounds to save her life. Then I hurried home to you!"

Liar's cocktails

So, to work properly, a convincing lie (and what's the point of telling any other kind?) needs to fit in with your particular circumstances. What you need are a range of ideas to blend like a cocktail into a tale of woe that proves:

(a) you are not really drunk, despite appearances, and

(b) absolves you from all responsibility for the state in which you are perceived to be.

Compiling a collection of great lies for every occasion is part of the vocation of every serious Drinking Man. It's a task that takes years of research and many sources: newspapers, magazines, books, jokes, pub talk, your mates, and so on.

Below are a few to get you started — blend them together with care and you'll be surprised at the results!

It's not my fault, because...*Researchers have discovered a gene at the root of alcoholism, which indicates that a liking for booze is at least in part an inherited disease and one over which an individual has little control.*

[The finding, published in the *Journal of the American Medical Association*, said in a study of the brains of alcoholics and non-alcoholics, the dopamine D2 receptor gene was present in almost all the drinkers, but in very few of the non-drinkers.

Since dopamine has been linked to craving and

pleasure-seeking behaviour, there is now a very strong case that people who love drinking simply cannot help themselves.]

It's not my fault, because...*I had to attend a symposium where the boss gave us a few glasses of this new product to sample. He's thinking of marketing it here and he'll need a ....* [insert the most believable and attractive job you might qualify for*] in the new division. So how could I rush home and refuse to help with sampling the new product?*

[No educated person could possibly deny your right to have a few drinks while having a day away from the office or an evening away from home to attend a symposium. That's because in the original Greek, symposium means literally "drinking together". It was used to describe an occasion when a group of Drinking Men would get together for a drink. To shift the blame for getting drunk from themselves, however, they first elected a leader who decided what and how much they should drink. Symposium protocol demanded members follow the leader's instructions at all times.]

It's not my fault, because...*The barman asked my opinion of the contents of this bottle of clear liquid. So as a favour to him I sampled it as I always do any drink — sparingly and in moderation. Except that it turned out to be a the world's most potent drink — a 98 percent (196 proof) potato vodka from Estonia.*

It's not my fault, because...*It was that half a bottle of cough mixture I had — I was only trying to cure a sore throat.*

It's not my fault, because...*My mother/aunt/grandmother [choose a relative you wife admires but who is not close enough to deny your story; someone dead is usually best] once told me the best cure for the flu is to gargle with .... [insert your favourite drink]. I was doing that on the way home when a huge mouthful slipped down my throat accidentally.*

It's not my fault, because...*I'd lost the cork — so I had to drink the whole bottle!*

It's not my fault, because...*You told me to spend less — so I tried to save money by cutting down on the amount of tonic with my gin!*

*It's not my fault, because...*The male menopause gives me hot flushes — which can only be cooled down with a cold beer.

*It's not my fault, because...*I was only trying to help you, trying to save our marriage. I saw this ad for an American brew and tested a few glasses to see if it would cure YOUR headaches, the kind you get at bedtime.

[This is what the ad said: "Selak's celebrated ale takes right hold of the vitals and elevates the soul. It opens the faculties, clears the canals of the heart, and strikes down the very bottom of contentedness."]

Hitting back

So what's your reply when your wife says: "I don't have any sympathy with a man who gets drunk every night!"

It's simple: "A man who can get drunk every night doesn't need any sympathy!"

Of course, it usually also works wonders when you arrive home drunk to tell her truthfully that you love her — and remind her that when she married you, by implication at least, she promised to stand by you "through thick and gin".

If all else fails...

Ask her to imagine YOU as a teetotaller! Tell her what that old Drinking Man's mate, the famous Henry Lawson, said in his hilarious short story, *The Boozer's Home*, about what happened to "a boozing mate's" wife when he finally succumbed to her pressure and gave up the grog:

"She loved and married a careless, good-natured, drinking scamp, and when he reformed and became a careful, hard-working man, and an honest and respected townsman, she was disappointed in him. He wasn't the man that won her heart when she was a girl..."

BOOZE v. WOMEN

☆ A drink does not get jealous when you enjoy a few more.

☆ A drink never has a headache.

☆ A drink doesn't get upset when you arrive home smelling of booze.

☆ A drink doesn't have a mother.

☆ You can share a drink with your mates.

☆ A frigid drink is usually your preferred choice.

☆ A drink looks the same the next morning.

☆ A drink never tries to change your driving habits.

☆ You can enjoy a drink while watching football or cricket.

☆ A drink never makes you lie and pretend you buy *Playboy* for the informative articles.

☆ A drink is always inviting and available - and **never** says no.

Drinker's I.Q. Test

No.4: DEPTH PERCEPTION

Which is the odd one out?

A

B

C

D

E

F

Answers on Page 189

A drunken motorist was stopped by the police whilst driving well over the speed limit. When asked, he explained he had drunk far too much to be able to drive, so he was hurrying home before he caused an accident.

KNOW YOUR BOOZE - PART 1

Beer, glorious Beer!

 SHAKESPEARE called it "a dish fit for a king," and Drinking Men around the world agree with heady delight, while quaffing their way through thousands of different brands of this golden brew.

ORIGINS

But where did beer or ale originate? Popular opinion has always pointed to Britain as the home of Beer, but historians have always thought this to be most unlikely.

In 1992, scientists working in Iran uncovered a jar at Goden Tepe which was carbon dated as coming from late 4,000 BC. The grooves of the jar were found to contain a substance known as calcium oxalate. This is the main component of 'beerstone' which is a deposit left by drinks brewed from barley. Although these oxalates could have come from other products, such as

rhubarb, it is considered most unlikely that the jar would have been used to store anything other than liquid - in other words, a fermented barley drink.

The brewers of this drink were Sumerians, one of the oldest literate civilisations. They employed a relatively complicated system of agriculture utilising irrigation to grow cereal crops including barley.

To convert the starch found in barley into a soluble form, the Sumerians probably made bread! A sourdough will have been added to the fresh barley and the resultant mixture made into loaves. These loaves, when broken up and added to water, would have fermented easily.

BEER IN BRITAIN

The fermented drink produced by the Sumerians would strictly have been called an 'ale'. Although the fermentation process is similar, to produce 'beer' requires the use of hops.

Cereals were being cultivated in Britain when the Romans conquered the country in 55BC. So it is likely that some of the barley being grown in this period was used to produce ale.

The modern word 'Ale' is probably derived from the Norse word 'Öl', which was used for their own Viking brew made from a large red berry found growing wild in many parts of Scandinavia.

In Saxon times the word 'beor' was used to describe inferior mead (fermented honey and water), but this word seemed to disappear from the language for around 500 years.

Hops were not introduced into Britain until the 1500's. They were initially grown by Flemish settlers in Kent. So it is likely that even the production of true 'beer' originated on the continent, probably in the Benelux region.

A CLOSER LOOK

So what is this amazing liquid we call beer and what about such close relatives such as ale and stout? Why are some beers light-coloured and others dark, some mind-blowingly potent and some extra mild, some old and others new? And how do master brewers create such an amazing range of tastes using four classic ingredients: barley, hops, yeast and water?

As described above, Beer is made from the brewing and fermentation of cereals, usually malted barley, and flavoured with hops to give it a bitter taste. Fungus yeast converts the sugars in the malted barley to alcohol. But if the alcohol content gets too high it kills the yeast, making it impossible to brew very strong beer. The most potent beer in the world is reputedly Roger & Out, with 16.9 per cent alcohol by volume (pbv).

Traditional beer and ale are top fermented (that is, the yeast floats on the top), while Lager (the most widely drunk beer in the world today) is bottom fermented. Lager which means storage was first brewed in a Bavarian monastery in the 14th century and because it needs a low fermentation temperature. Until the invention of refrigeration, lagers were brewed next to lakes that froze over in winter. Lagers are light coloured, have a medium hop flavour, dry taste, high carbonation and an alcohol content usually between three and four pbv.

Top fermented beers, which are particularly popular in Britain, include ale, stout and porter.

Stout was originally brewed and called stoutt as a thick and very potent drink which was served like a liqueur in small fluted glasses. Women loved this drink, because it was supposed to keep their shape in the way men then thought attractive. It helped them maintain a kind of buxom stoutness which artists like Rubens and Rembrandt painted with such delight. The drink was gradually thinned down into the stout we know today, perhaps to keep up with female fashion for a thinner form. Stout gets its dark colour from roasted barley or malt which is included with the normal malt and other ingredients before mashing.

Think of stout and most people today think of Guin-

**A pub scene last century ... with German beers such
as Bock, famed for their purity, already very popular**

ness, Ireland's most famous export which, it is claimed,
gets its soft and special taste from certain springs in the
County Kildare, before being allowed to mature for a
year in oaken vats.

Ale and Stout have a stronger, more hoppy flavour
than Lager and their alcohol content usually ranges between 4-6.5 pbv.

In Germany, since 1615, only barley, hops, yeast and
water have been used for brewing hundreds of different
varieties of beer, following the promulgation of the
Pure Beer Law by Count William IV of Bavaria.

Not so in countries such as Australia. A New South
Wales Act of 1850 aimed to curb some of the worst

concoctions which were being sold as beer. A brewer faced a then substantial fine of £200 and confiscation of his stock if he should add to his brew any vitriol, coculus indicus, nux vomica, tobacco, opium, aloes, copperas ,faba amara or any extract or preparation thereof...   And if you're wondering about nux vomica... it's another term for strychnine!

Other additives used in the past were also quite detrimental to the health of heavy drinkers, such as cobalt salts used in the 1960s (but now abandoned) to improve beer's foaming qualities.

Additives allowed for beer today are: propylene glycol alginate, sulphur dioxide, ascorbic acid or erythorbic acid, caramel, tannic acid, papain, bromelin and ficin.

Today there is a big trend towards pure beer, which relies on traditional ingredients and the brewmaster, rather than additives, to achieve great taste. The champions of this cause are The Campaign for Real Ale (CAMRA), started by a group of friends in Britain in 1971 out of enthusiasm for cask-conditioned ale. CAMRA has now turned into a respected consumer organisation and is regularly consulted by the media on all subjects beer.

How very civilised

Every beer lover knows the golden brew is the most civilised drink on earth — and now there's anthropological proof for this obvious fact.

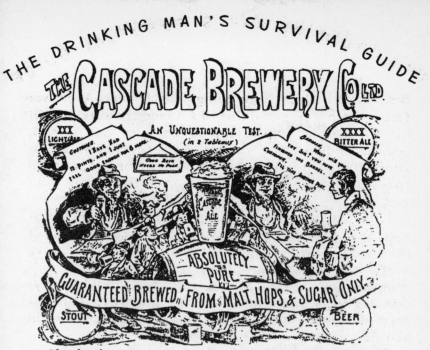

Absolutely pure ... Tasmania's Cascade Beer last century

It was the discovery of home brewing, about 10,000 years ago, that led our ancestors to settle down and start cultivating crops, according to Dr Solomon Katz of the University of Pennsylvania's Anthropology Department.

He said the event that "primed the pump" of civilisation was the accidental discovery by prehistoric humans that wild wheat and barley soaked in water to make gruel, if left in the open air, did not spoil.

Instead, natural yeast in the air converted it to a dark, bubbling brew that make whoever drank it feel good. On top of that, the brew made people robust: at the time, it was second only to animal protein as a nutritional source.

Dr Katz said this combination of mood-altering and

nutritional properties would have been incentive enough to cause neolithic hunter-gatherers in the Near East to begin cultivating the grains.

He pointed out that the oldest known recipe for brewing beer was found on a Sumerian clay tablet produced over 7000 years ago.

Beer was the most popular drink in ancient Egypt, with peasants and workers building the pyramids receiving two jugs of beer and four loaves of bread a day. Beer was also left in tombs to refresh the dead on their journey to the underworld.

Recent excavations have revealed Queen Nefertiti's temple, about 3000 years ago, had its own brewery. Ancient texts and wall paintings suggest there were several different beers, ranging from thick ales full of gruel to those of a finer texture.

Wall paintings also reveal the presence even then of Drinking Men — courtiers vomiting after having to much beer.

Egyptian priests had a great old time in the temples — because they not only tucked into all the food left as offerings for the gods, but the drink as well. And there certainly was plenty of that — the pharoah Ramses alone offered up the grand total of 466,303 pitchers of beer to the gods in the 12th century BC.

The ancient art of quaffing

A good beer — and that surely includes your favourite drop — deserves to be served at the right temperature and in a way that best brings out its full flavour.

So, unless your thirst is desperate, don't drink straight from the bottle or can. Instead, use a glass or

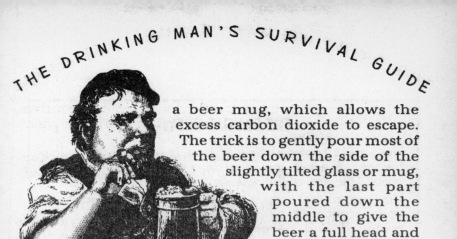

a beer mug, which allows the excess carbon dioxide to escape. The trick is to gently pour most of the beer down the side of the slightly tilted glass or mug, with the last part poured down the middle to give the beer a full head and to enhance its bouquet.

When serving home brew (or other bottle fermented brews such as Cooper's Sparkling Ale), pour with great care to avoid any of the sediment getting into the glass. Here's how to do it:

✔ Line up the glasses and carefully remove the bottle cap.

✔ Tilt the first glass, then pour the beer slowly down the side, bringing the glass vertical as it fills up.

✔ Put down the full glass but keep the bottle tilted.

✔ Repeat with the other glasses until just before you reach the sediment, then stop.

Experts say the *ideal temperature* for serving Lager is 5.5°C; for all-malt beers 8°C to 10°C; for ale and Stout (including Guinness) 12.7°C. An ice-cold beer may sound good, but freezing it is one certain way to spoil a brew. When an all-malt beer is served below 7°C. it will develop "chill haze"; this makes the beer hazy, but will usually clear as the temperature rises.

THE DEVIL'S BREW!

The wowser point of view of beer is summed up by this description which appeared in a temperance magazine around the turn of the century:

The use of beer is found to produce a species of degeneration of all the organs; profound and deceptive fatty deposits, diminished circulation, conditions of congestion and perversion of functional activity, local inflammation of both the liver and kidneys are constantly present. Intellectually a stupor amounting almost to paralysis arrests the reason, changing all the higher faculties into a mere animalism, sensual, selfish, sluggish, varied only with paroxysms of anger that are senseless and brutal. In appearance the beer drinker may be the picture of health, but in reality he is almost incapable of resisting disease. A slight injury, a severe cold, or a shock of the body or mind, will commonly provoke an acute disease ending fatally. Compared with inebriates who drink different kinds of alcohol, he is more incurable and more generally diseased. The constant use of beer every day gives the system no recuperation, but lowers the vital forces.

Weird world of beer

 IF YOU find politics dry, why not liven it up with a drop of beer? It's easy — just start your own political party whose main platform is encouraging the drinking of beer!

Which is exactly what happened in the famous Czech brewery town of Pilsen (that's where Pilsner comes from) when the nation's first free elections in 40 years were called in 1991.

"The main objective of the party is to decrease the price of beer while increasing its quality and consumption," a local newspaper reported.

And that in a country where, at the time, a bottle of the high-quality Pilsner Urquell cost a mere 25 cents!

The party, known in Czech as the *Strana Pratel Piva*,

or "Friends of Beer," claimed at least 10,000 supporters. "We ask all people who like Czech beer to support our demands by a manifestative gluttony on any day in any pub," noted the party's official declaration.

Sadly, it's quaffing candidates failed to win a single seat in the elections. Some observers say party members were so busy drinking they either forgot or were incapable of voting on the day.

In 1436 a Royal writ ordered the Sheriffs of London to proclaim that "the drink called beere is a notable, healthy and temperate drink" — and anyone who said otherwise faced severe punishment.

Beer has had some strange uses over the centuries, indeed. A letter of Pope Gregory to Archbishop Nidrosietisi, of Iceland, shows that in the 13th Century ale was so popular that some communities even used it to baptise their children!

Wrote the wowser Pope: "... since the heart ought to be born again of water and the Holy Spirit, those ought not to be considered as duly baptised who have been baptised in ale."

And in Norman times in Merrie Olde England, during the King's travels through the country, the servants even washed the horses' feet in ale, much to the disgust of thirsty locals whose entire beer supply was sometimes used up in this extravagance.

Need an excuse to have a beer? Then why not blow your money — and get your mates to stage a "Bede-ale" to restore your fortunes!

Bede-ale was a medieval male custom very much like the Australian concept of mateship. If an honest man suffered a financial setback, through no fault of his own, the law allowed his friends to drink him back to prosperity!

The publican, by law, had to hand over a certain percentage of all the money the drinkers spent during this Bede-ale session to the victim. The bigger the financial loss, of course, the longer — and drunker — the party. And, because it was permitted by law, no wife dared complain!

Other old customs involving beer drinking were Bid-Ales, Bride-Ales, Give-Ales, Cuckoo-Ales, Help-Ales, Tithe-Ales, Leet-Ales, Lamb-Ales, Midsummer-Ales, Scot-Ales, and Wedden-Ales.

Bride-Ale was the English custom of the bride selling ale on the wedding day, for which she received any sum or present which her friends chose to give her.

And what parties these weddings were! One account from 1545 notes matter-of-factly:

"When they came home from the church, then beginneth excess of eatyng and drynking, and as much is waisted in one daye as were sufficient for the two newe-married folkes half a yeare to lyve upon."

Four centuries ago, being an official Ale Taster was a job many beer lovers thirsted after. And no wonder: you could drink officially all day, then get paid in beer!

Noted one writer in 1617: "John Shule had a patent from Arthur Lake, Bishop of Bath and Wells, and Vice-Chancellor of Oxford, for the office of ale-taster [to the University] and the making and assizing of barrels of beer. The office of ale tasting requires that he go to every ale-brewer that day they brew, according to their courses, and taste their ale; for which, his ancient fee is one gallon of strong ale and two gallons of small wort, worth a penny."

Who was the greatest beer drinker in history? When it comes to *free* beers, there's no doubt the honour goes to a Pom named Jedediah Buxton, who throughout his life meticulously tallied up every beer anyone had ever bought him since he started drinking — at the age of 12!

Sixty years or so later the total came to an amazing 5116 pints, equal to about 10,000 tinnies. Jedediah

"YOU'LL NEVER MISS THE WATER"

claimed he could down a pint with only one breath —
and won his free beers from those curious to see how
many pints he could drink without losing his breath.

Have you ever pigged out on beer? Then you'll have
some sympathy with the unfortunate porcines
belonging to home-brewing parson Rev. John
Woodforde in 1765, who wrote with some
astonishment in his diary:

"Brewed a vessell of strong Beer today. My two large
Piggs, by drinking some Beer grounds taken out of one
of my Barrels today, got so amazingly drunk by it, that
they were not able to stand and appeared like dead
things almost, and so remained all night from
dinner-time today. I never saw Piggs so drunk in my
life, I slit their ears for them without feeling..."

The next day the saga continued:

"My two Piggs are still unable to walk yet, but they
are better than they were yesterday. They tumble
about the yard and can be no means stand at all steady

yet. Only this afternoon did they become tolerably sober..."

How the rector fared after drinking the actual brew that produced such potent grains is not recorded. Although his handwriting for a week was decidedly shaky...

Queenslander Graham Howard's Laidly Gold wheat beer is a real beauty bottler — literally so! It took 418.25 litres of the golden brew to fill the world's largest beer bottle at the Laidley Tourist Festival — and win Graham a spot in the *Guinness Book of Records*. The huge bottle, made specially for the occasion, stood 2.11 metres tall and had a circumference of 1.64 metres.

Graham's other pure wheat beers have such lip-smacking names as Brewhouse Old Bounty Ale and Settlers' Extra Stout.

In ancient Mesopotamia Queen Shu-Bad thought so highly of beer that she would drink it only one way — by sipping it through a straw made of solid gold.

During the reign of Queen Elizabeth I, beer was divided into single beer, or small beer, double beer, double-double beer, and dagger ale, which was particularly sharp and strong. Good Queen Bess, who served huge quantities of beer and ale at all Royal functions, drank her own special Royal Brew which was said to be so strong that no one else in the household could handle it.

Sex and the Drinking Man

THERE'S a Sumerian proverb which says: "No drunkenness without beer, no pregnancy without sex." Sadly, however, for many a Drinking Man, sex and beer (or any other alcoholic drink) often simply don't mix, because drink "provokes the desire, but it takes away the performance".

That's from Shakespeare, obviously a red-blooded Drinking Man himself, who adds: "Therefore much drink may be said to be an equivocater with lechery: it makes him, and it mars him; it sets him on, and it takes him off; it persuades him, and disheartens him; makes him stand to, and not stand to..."

In plain English, what the Bard is talking about, of course, is that bane of the Drinking Man: *Brewer's Droop*.

It's been a problem since the first man took his first drink and then looked at a woman with lust in his eyes. This inability to perform occupied the minds of thinking men (and Drinking Men) from the earliest times. The famous ancient Greek philosopher

COME ALONG, SIR — HAVEN'T YOU GOT
A PAIR OF BOOBS TO GO HOME TO ?!

Aristotle blamed it all on the heat:

"Why cannot the drunken have sexual intercourse? Is it because one part of the body must be hotter than the rest, which cannot be the case with the drunken owing to their excessive heat? So the heat caused by movement is quenched, being heated by the surrounding heat.

"Or is it because the lower parts require to be heated, but wine naturally travels upwards, so that it produces heat there and withdraws it from the other part?

"After food men are least inclined to intercourse, so that they recommend a large breakfast but a light dinner; for when food is undigested there is an upward travel of heat and moisture; but when digested downwards: and

the production of semen is due to heat and moisture.

"The weary emit semen at night because weariness is warm and wet; if, then, there is any waste product in this place, emission occurs. It is for the same reason that it happens with those whose health is bad. Similarly also it occurs with those who are frightened or dying."

That's the bad news. Here is the good: a brewery in France (where else?) claims it is on the verge of developing a brew that will allow Drinking Men to guzzle with gusto — and still be in the mood for love!

A heady announcement said the brewery had started tests on a beer, said to contain natural aphrodisiacs, that does not affect the Drinking Man's ability for making love.

It said the beer was being tested under strict medical control by 400 drinkers. Explained Technical Director Marc Arbogast: "It is not a product for Don Juan or marathon love makers, but is meant for men who have experienced sexual inhibitions."

Amazingly, the beer is not likely to be very potent (as you would expect for it to release all those inhibitions), but is under development in the form of a mild barley brew with only about 2.5 per cent alcohol, about the same as a typical low-alcohol lager.

"Alcohol is known for its effect of sapping virility and this should reverse the effects," the director added.

So where can you buy this amazing brew? Nowhere yet — and the fact that this amazing good news story was published on April Fool's Day should give you some idea of when it is likely to be available. Although the brewery, of course, denied strenuously that it was playing a practical joke on beer-loving lovers.

Now, before we are accused of being sexist (a far-fetched accusation, indeed, because women are not Drinking Men nor do they suffer from *Brewer's Droop*), here's some sexy news about women and booze:

Gwen, you smell so, so.... intoxicating

It is a fact of human nature that females use alcohol in the form of perfume to attract men (even though they usually object to men who smell of alcohol). In the case of the emperor moth, according to German scientists, the male can detect the alcohol-based sex scent of a virgin female from as far away as 11 km!

In a recent issue, *Pageant* magazine, under the headline *Distinguished Doctors Name the Eight Foods That Spark Sexual Desire*, reported:

"Peculiarly, of the commonly available foods, beer is the most likely to give women a boost in basic femininity... The hop is one of the few foods actually containing estrogens..."

Is your name Denis or Dennis? Then you're in luck — you're named after the Greek God of Wine, Dionysus (also called Bacchus by the Romans). But if your wife or lover's name is Denise — beware!

Dionysus invented the religious sex orgy in ancient Greece, a religion enthusiastically embraced by the Romans. The god's female followers (those early Denise's) developed a reputation for licentiousness that terrified every Roman Drinking Man.

On the many feast days of Bacchus, his buxom followers drank large amounts of wine, often laced with milk and honey, as they worked themselves into a sexual frenzy. They would tear animals apart, eating them raw — and then abducted any man they could find to use for their own amusement!

GOURMET: *A man invited for an evening of wine, women and song - and asks what kind of wine.*

Drinker's  I.Q. Test

No.5: CRUNCH TIME

If a bag of Salt & Vinegar crisps costs you 60 cents, and the bag contains 25g, which of the following would work out more expensive than your crisps per tonne?

A. Aluminium

B. Copper

C: Potatoes

D. Sugar

E. Nickel

F. Gas Oil

G. Live pigs

Answers on Page 189

"Doctor, doctor, I feel like a glass of gin!"
"Try taking a little tonic!"

The barman asked a new customer why he was holding two schooner glasses in front of his eyes. The customer explained that he was trying to make a spectacle of himself!

Pub talk

A BAR, they say, is a place where you get wet change and dry martinis ... and much, much more. Every Drinking Man has at least one favourite pub: your "home away from home" where you're always welcome to enjoy a drink or ten in convivial company — and no one to nag you.

When it comes to pub talk, the merits of different drinks and different pubs are favourite topics among Drinking Men the world over. Here are some unusual bar-related nuggets for you to mention casually next time someone says, "Have you heard about the pub where...?"

Until upstaged a few years ago by the Canadians, Australia boasted the world's longest bar — a 90-metre drinking haven in the Working Man's Club at Mildura, Victoria.

First opened in 1895 as a bastion of the Riverland town's Drinking Men, it finally admitted women 85 years later — only a few months after the first female was employed as a barmaid.

The T-shaped bar's 27 permanent taps have been the scene of amazing "tap crawl" challenges, involving having a beer from each one in turn at speed.

According to the *Guinness Book of Records*, the world's longest permanent bar today is the 103.6-metre bar in "Lulu's Roadhouse", Kitchener, Ontario, Canada, which opened in April 1984.

The Yankee claim to fame in the big bar stakes is that at a saloon in Oregon named Erickson's. From 1883 until just before prohibition, it boasted a permanent bar 208.48 metres long that ran continuously around and across the main saloon, with beer at 5 cents a glass.

To keep the multitude in check, the pub employed some tough bouncers indeed, the most famous of whom was "Jumbo" Reilly, who weighed in at 23 stone (322 pounds) and resembled "an ill-natured orangutan".

Australia's — and probably the world's — most unusual drinking establishment is the *Left Hand Club* in Whyalla.

It's a place where sometimes right is wrong — and if you don't know what that means you could get left with an empty change pocket.

The South Australian social club was formed in 1942 with a weird bunch of rules aimed at raising money for the war effort and local charities.

On any day but a Wednesday visitors to this unorthodox club discover to their cost exactly what the name means — each time you touch your drink with your right hand (a pretty natural way of doing things for right-handed Drinking Men), a "fines box" appears under your nose demanding yet another coin.

Guests and members are equally liable for fines if they break the rules.

The first of which (according to the rule book), is: "Ours is a Left Hand Club and a member must, at all times, excepting Wednesday (Right Hand Day), handle his own drinking vessel with the Left Hand."

"'Handle' does not necessarily mean lift or drink. Any member detected touching his own drinking vessel in any way with the wrong hand is guilty of an offence!"

Then, to take the sting out of it, the rule book adds: "The primary object of all fines is to assist local distress and members are directed to pay and play the game at all times."

It takes a while, but even confirmed right-handers eventually come to grips with southpaw imbibing — which is why the cunning rule makers decided that on

Wednesdays "a member must not touch his own drinking vessel with the Left Hand".

And giving your left hand to be ambidextrous is not enough ...

☆ Between noon and 2pm and between 5pm and 6pm, certain other rules apply as well:

☆ Monday is *No Borrow Day* when members must not ask for matches, cigarettes, the time of day, or in any way beg or ask a favour from fellow members.

☆ On Tuesday, known as *Yes Day*, members must not use the words "Yes", "Yeah", "Uum", or nod the head indicating the affirmative when in the company of club members.

☆ On Thursday, swearing or blaspheming in any way means yet another offering for the fines box.

☆ Friday, again, is a *No Day*, when members may not use the word "No", or shake their head to indicate the negative.

The first known barmaids in the world worked in ancient Babylon, where the penalty for pouring a short beer was death by drowning.

The ancient Egyptians, who wisely saw alcohol as a sacred gift to mankind from the goddess Isis, brewed an impressive range of beers, using barley steeped in water and fermented with bread crumbs and natural yeasts floating about in the air.

Almost 4000 years ago they were serving these brews in comfortable beer gardens, forerunners of the modern pub.

Australia's narrowest pub, pictured above, can be seen in the heart of Kalgoorlie, where it did brisk business between 1899 and 1924. A mere 3.35 metres wide, the British Arms was strategically placed opposite the busy Hannan Street railway station, which meant it quenched the thirst of miners both coming to and leaving the fabulously rich West Australian goldfield.

After losing its liquor licence, the British Arms served as a boarding house until it was turned into the present Golden Mile Museum in 1968. Much of the rip-roaring history of the area is still preserved there — but, sadly, you can no longer get a drink.

More beer is sold daily at the Mathaser bar in Bayerstrasse 5, Munich, Germany, than anywhere else in the world — 48,000 litres! Established in 1829, the bar fell victim to World War II, but was rebuilt by 1955 and now seats 5500 Drinking Men (and a few women) at a time.

And while in Germany — barmaid Rosie Schedelbauer, carrying five full beersteins in every hand, dashed 15 metres to a world record in a mere four seconds in 1981.

In New York last century, determined Drinking Men with a big thirst (and big mouths) but not much money could get a big drink in a most unusual way.

Bars in the Bowery connected hoses to beer kegs, then allowed anyone who paid one cent to slurp up as much beer as he could *without drawing breath!*

According to contemporary reports, some expert drinkers could hold their breath for as long as *two minutes* while they sucked and sucked and sucked and sucked!

Great things happen in bars, so every Drinking Man has a duty to spend lots of time there in case he misses out on some historic event.

☆ The US Marine Corps, one of the world's most elite fighting units, was founded in 1775 — inside a pub in Philadelphia called the Tun Tavern. Marines have been known for their drinking and killing prowess ever since.

☆ The American Declaration of Independence was

Bar scene last century ... weird drinks on offer

written by Thomas Jefferson while quaffing beer at the Indian Queen pub in Philadelphia.

☆ The "Star Spangled Banner" was written by Francis Scott Key while doing the same at the Fountain Inn in Baltimore.

No one can blame the regulars for having a whale of a time at their watering hole in Wonthaggi, Victoria. To enter the Wonthaggi Hotel, you first have to pass through the jawbones of a 23-metre whale washed up on the nearby beach in 1923. The jawbones form a massive archway at the main entrance.

Talk about ghoulish behaviour! New Orleans last century boasted a pub which was an exact replica of an above-ground burial vault!

WINE CASKET

The Conclave Saloon's barmen were dressed as undertakers, booze was kept in bottles shaped like coffins, and drinks on offer were advertised on marble slabs shaped like tombstones. But you needed real money to drink!

BAR SIGNS

The customer is always tight   *Thirst come thirst served*

How to get a beer in ...

THERE are more shapes and sizes of drinking vessels for beer than for any other beverages in the world - and rightly so, because beer, after all, is the world's favourite drink. But that home of lager drinkers, Australia, do take things a bit far when it comes to asking for a 'beer' in a pub.

They have a dazzling range of names for various sizes of beer — and they not only vary from State to State, but the same name in one State often means a completely different thing in another.

For instance, ask for a schooner in New South Wales and you'll get a respectable 15 ounces (425ml) of your favourite brew. In South Australia a schooner is only 10 ounces (285ml), but a pint is 15 ounces (425ml) — unlike the New South Wales pint which is 20 ounces (568ml).

It all gets confusing depending on which State (and what state) you're in, so to help you order like a native no matter where you happen to be, here's a quick and easy Drinking Man's guide:

New South Wales and A.C.T.

Pint	(20 ounces/568ml)
Schooner	(15 ounces/425ml)
Middy	(10 ounces/285ml)
Seven	(7 ounces/200ml)
Pony	(5 ounces/140ml)

Victoria

Schooner	(15 ounces/425ml)
Pot	(10 ounces/285ml)
Glass	(7 ounces/200ml)
Small Glass	(6 ounces/170ml)
Pony	(5 ounces/140ml)

Queensland

Pot	(10 ounces/285ml)
Beer	(7 ounces/200ml)
Five	(5 ounces/140ml)

South Australia

Pint	(15 ounces/425ml)
Schooner	(10 ounces/285ml)
Butcher	(7 ounces/200ml)
Pony	(5 ounces/140ml)

"IT HAD TO HAPPEN — THEY PAY THE BAR STAFF PEANUTS!"

Tasmania

"Ten" or Pot	(10 ounces/285ml)
"Eight"	(8 ounces/225ml)
"Six"	(6 ounces/170ml)
Small Beer	(4 ounces/115ml)

Northern Territory

Schooner	(15 ounces/425ml)
Handle	(10 ounces/285ml)
"Seven"	(7 ounces/200ml)

Western Australia

Pot	(20 ounces/575ml)
Schooner	(15 ounces/425ml)
Middy	(10 ounces/285ml)
Glass	(7 ounces/200ml)
Bobbie	(6 ounces/170ml)
Pony	(5 ounces/140ml)
Shetland	(4 ounces/115ml)

A mug's game?

Germans have a huge range of beer steins, the biggest of which holds four litres of amber fluid. The closet we Brits come to that is the 'jar' or 'mug'. But have you ever wondered why we call it a "mug"?

If you've ever seen a Toby jug, you'll guess the answer. The term started in 18th century England where patrons brought their own mugs to alehouses — which soon became known as mughouses — and left them there. Each mug was uniquely identified with its owner, so anyone's face (his or her unique feature) became known as his or her "mug".

A tumbler today is associated with drinking water rather than beer, yet it s name is directly related to the golden brew. In Anglo-Saxon days drinking horns were used by beer-loving warriors — and tradition demanded the ale or beer had to be drained with one gulp.

To stop anyone cheating, the horns had rounded

bottoms so that when you put one down it would tumble — and spill any ale left inside for all to see. The first glass glasses followed this round-bottomed pattern and so became known as "tumblers" — and the name stuck even when they acquired flat bottoms.

The closest we now have to a drinking horn is the Ale-yard — a trumpet-shaped glass vessel, exactly a yard in length, with a closed narrow end which is expanded into a large ball.

It holds little more than a pint, and when filled with ale or beer the challenge is to empty the entire yard without taking it away from your mouth. This is far from easy, as any rugby club champion beer drinker or drunken student eager to prove their manhood will attest. For, so long as the tube contains beer, it flows out smoothly, but when air reaches the bulb it displaces the beer with a splash, startling the drinker so that he involuntarily withdraws his mouth. The result? Cold beer all over!

If you thought a yard of ale was hard going, try sampling a Wager or Puzzle fug. In the 17th century these strange beer mugs were great favourites at country inns.

Puzzle fugs usually had many spouts, from most of which it was difficult to drink – owing to holes in the neck. Those in the know used to slurp up the liquor through a secret passage in the hollow handle or through one spout or nozzle — if the drinker had enough fingers to stop up the other spouts and holes during the operation!

Drinker's  I.Q. Test

No.6: OOPS!

You can feel a warm sensation down your left leg. Have you ...

A. Stood next to the fire?

B. Provided companionship for a lonely dog?

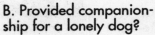

C. Forgotten your way to the toilets?

D. Spilt your drink?

Answers on Page 189

Did you hear about the man who fell into a very large vat of whisky?

He drowned after three hours. Of course, it could have been quicker, but he kept getting out to go to the toilet.

KNOW YOUR BOOZE - PART 2

Firewater: Spirits and liqueurs

Water is an excellent drink if taken with the right spirit, that hero of every Drinking Man, W.C. Fields, once remarked. Distillation to create "firewater" by separating alcohol from water through heating has been known for thousands of years and was recorded by the ancient Egyptians and the ancient Chinese, Greeks and Romans.

Known in Latin as *aqua vitae* (water of life), distilled spirits were used for both intoxicating and medicinal purposes from the outset. Hippocrates, the father of medicine, even suggested spirits should be used regularly to purify water.

There are a great many spirits available which every Drinking Man should endeavour, at some stage, to sample. Here's some basic information (and a few very

odd but true facts) about the main spirits and liqueurs
to set those taste buds tingling.

SCOTCH WHISKY

There's a true old saying: "No one cares how bad your
English is as long as your Scotch is good."

Whisky is made from ripened and dried barley. This
is steeped in spring water in tanks called "steeps" for
between 52 and 62 hours. The grain is then spread out
on concrete floors and allowed to sprout. This
germinating grain is then placed on a sieve and dried
over a peat fire in the kiln — and it is the oily smoke
of the peat that gives Scotch its distinct smoky flavour.

After being screened, the dried malt is ground up

Highland toast ... with Scotch, of course

to release the sugar, then mashed in large mash-tuns using warm water which converts all the starches into sugar. The resulting liquid is called wort. When yeast is added in fermenting vats, a beer-like brew called wash is created.

Next stop is the very important wash still, an enormous copper "pot" with a pipe leading out of the top. As the wash is heated, the alcohol is the first to evaporate and is carried off by this pipe. This alcohol (known as low wines), is again distilled before it yields whisky.

The new whisky is diluted with water to the required alcoholic strength, or "proof". Proof is the percentage of alcohol and always double the true figure; thus, 80% proof denotes 40% alcohol. This diluted whisky is placed in wood barrels and allowed to mature to perfection.

It will never be certain whether the Scots or the Irish invented whisky; what is sure is that the name derives from Gaelic and means "the water of life".

Certainly the Scots used whisky to help them warm up during the bitter winters, with Samuel Johnson noting that "As soon as he appears in the morning, a man of the Hebrides swallows a glass of whisky"! He stressed, however, that he rarely saw drunk Scotsmen, in the morning or at any other time.

There's a single-malt Scotch bottled in Gloucestershire with the unappealing name *Original Oldbury Sheep Dip*. The story goes that it was named this way to allow canny highland farmers to write off their whiskey from their taxes as farming expenses. Farmers, naturally, have denied this.

Famous Highland malts include The Balvenie,

"I'VE FOUND A PERFECT WAY OF CONQUERING FEAR OF THE BIG PISTE — FIVE DOUBLE WHISKYS!"

Cardhu, The Glenlivet, Glenfiddich, Glen Grant, Glenmorangie, The MaCallan, and Tomatin, while the best-known Lowland malts are Auchentoshan and Rosebank. Single-malt scotch is best enjoyed neat (like an after-dinner cognac) or diluted with a small quantity of water.

Single malt Scotches, with their highly individual characteristics, are expensive and not as popular as blended Scotch whisky.

By the end of the 19th century, blended Scotches appeared for the first time and today the vast majority of single malt Scotch is blended with grain-based Scotch whiskies to make a drink that with a lighter and smoother character. A blended whisky can contain as many as 40 different varieties.

Today, there are more than 2500 kinds of scotch made in four regions of Scotland: the Highlands around Speyside; the islands (mainly Islay, Skye, Jura and Orkney); the Lowlands, close to Glasgow; and Campbeltown in the south-west.

More than 70 million nine-litre cases of whisky are exported from Scotland each year. Until they are despatched, they are kept in huge hanger-like bonded warehouses, which are regularly checked by customs.

IRISH WHISKEY

Legend has it that St. Patrick taught the Irish how to make a fiery liquor called *poteen* (literally "in the pot") from malted barley — which inevitably led to the creation of whiskey.

Like Scotch, Irish whiskey is distilled from a fermented mash of barley grains, but tastes completely different because it is not dried in a sieve, but on a solid floor which prevents the smoke flavour reaching the malt. All Irish whiskey is matured for at least seven years.

You can drink Irish whiskey straight, on ice or with a mixer. It's probably most used in Britain as the main ingredient in Irish coffee.

To make Irish coffee, pour 60ml of Irish whiskey into a mug of coffee, add sugar to taste and stir, then pour thick cream over the back of a spoon onto the coffee to form a thick layer. Do not stir, but sip the coffee through the cream.

On St Patrick's Day, surprise the Irish Drinking Men

you know with a delightful (and very green) *St. Pat's Cocktail.* You'll need

>*45ml Irish whiskey*
>*Crème de menthe*
>*Green Chartreuse*

To the whiskey, add 3 dashes of Crème de menthe and six dashes of Chartreuse. Shake with ice. Strain into chilled cocktail glass.

AMERICAN WHISKEY

Early settlers in the New World sought to ease their harsh pioneer life with spirits fermented and distilled from wild fruits and vegetables. Early moonshine' spirits made with corn or rye are the ancestors of today's American whiskeys.

Kentucky humorist Irvin S. Cobb once likened his State's famous "corn likker" to the wrath of God. "It smells like gangrene rising in a mildewed silo," he added. "When you absorb a deep swig of it, you have all the sensations of having swallowed a lighted kerosene lamp. It will stop your pocket watch, snap your suspenders and crack your glass eye right across."

American whiskey is made in much the same way as Scotch, except that is is matured in newly charred barrels made of white oak. It is the charring that creates the distinctive colour and adds to the unique flavour.

Bourbon is so called not because it has any relationship with the French royal house of Bourbon, but because it was first distilled by the Reverend Elijah Craig in the Bourbon County of Kentucky. It is distilled from at least 51% maize, while Rye whiskey is made from at least 51% rye grain.

Southern Comfort is a very popular, but quite unusual, bourbon — because it is blended with peach liqueur. It developed from a Missouri cocktail of bourbon and peach liqueur last century which proved so popular it became a bottled drink.

Sour Mash whiskey is made by the sour-mash yeasting process.

Tennessee Whiskey, of which Jack Daniel is probably best known (and considered by many as the best of its kind), receives its unique taste from being filtered slowly through fine sugar-maple charcoal in vats as high as a house, before being aged in charred-oak barrels for at least four years.

Canadian whisky (spelt like its Scotch counterpart) is made from a mixture of rye, corn wheat and barley malt. Thus it is popularly known as *rye*, although there is no law which stipulates the exact proportions of rye to these other grains. After maturing in new white-oak casks or charred old bourbon barrels for at least three years, all Canadian whisky is blended, with about 10% pure rye whisky usually added at this stage.

BRANDY

*Have ready a bottle of brandy, because I
always feel like drinking that heroic drink...*

— HERMAN MELVILLE

Brandy is one of the most popular spirits in the world. Made by distilling wine or fermented grape juice, like wine the finest brandies come from France, in the form of Cognac and Armagnac.

It was during the Middle Ages that enterprising French winemakers first converted low-quality wines, caused by poor grape harvests, into delightful brandies.

Yet the name is derived from the Dutch *brandewijn* (burnt wine) — a reference to the heat applied to distill wine into brandy. The dark colour comes more from caramel and is also produced by ageing. In Australia, brandy by law has to be aged for at least two years before it can be sold. To be called "Old", it must be aged for five years, while "Very Old" requires 10 years of maturation.

The term **Cognac** is used to describe brandy made in the Cognac region of France, where more than 70,000 small farmers grow the white grapes used in its manufacture. It takes 10 barrels of wine to make one barrel of brandy, which is aged for at least two years (but often much longer) in oak casks which provide the distinctive amber colour.

The world's oldest brandy is **Armanac**, which was first distilled in 1411 in the French province of Gascony. It is matured in black oak casks and has a drier taste and more pungent aroma than cognac.

ODD BUT TRUE: Ever heard of ant-brandy? A prominent historian noted last century: "It is well known that the Swedes, whose propensity for strong drink is well known, flavour their brandy by distilling it with a large species of the black ant. These insects contain resin, an oil, and an acid, which are highly valued for the flavour and potency which they import to the brandy. They are found in abundance in the bottom of fir-trees, in small, round hills, and are taken in that state for use."

GIN

Invented in Holland for medicinal purposes in the 17th century, the Dutch named this grain spirit *genever* (after the juniper berry, gin's main flavouring ingredient). Other flavouring ingredients used to make gin include coriander, angelica root, cinnamon, dried orange contribute, lemon, liquorice, and bitter almonds. Caraway is still an important ingredient in Dutch gin.

English soldiers brought gin back from European wars and, when during a trade war with France wine and brandy was taxed heavily, gin became the nation's favourite drink.

Like vodka, it does not have to be aged but can be drunk the day it is distilled. That made it even cheaper to produce. To give this already fiery liquid an added kick, the ingredients of the original London Dry gin at times included sulphuric acid and oil of turpentine.

The quality was appalling but it appealed to the masses because the price was very low: to get drunk, as one pub sign proclaimed, you needed only a penny;

for two, you could get "Dead Drunk"! Hogarth's famous painting *Gin Lane* (above) all too clearly illustrates the misery gin caused among the London poor.

Dry gin (often called London Dry) is used for

cocktails such as the Singapore Sling because it is much blander than Hollands gin. Other types are **Sloe gin** (a liqueur created by steeping ripe sloe berries in gin; **Plymouth gin** (more strongly flavoured than the Dry type); and **Old Tom gin** (a sweetened variety).

Today most used as a basis for cocktails, gin is also popular as a long cool drink served with tonic water. Gin-and-tonic became a popular British drink in India when adding gin made the quinine in tonic water easier to stomach. Today's tonic water still contains some quinine.

VODKA

Distilled for at least 600 years in Russia from fermented grain mash at very high proof, the name vodka aptly means "Little Water" because it is an unflavoured, neutral spirit purified through vegetable charcoal. In parts of Poland and Russia, potatoes are sometimes used to make vodka.

Unlike almost all other popular spirits, vodka does not need maturing but tastes exactly the same the day it is distilled and purified than it does years later.

When vodka became popular in America and other western countries in the early 1950s, advertisers cashed in on the fact that it leaves no odour on the drinker's breath, with one popular brand being promoted under the slogan: "Wifey won't know!" Another popular slogan of the time was: "It leaves you breathless".

Russians traditionally drink vodka neat, ice cold, and in one gulp, but it is more popular in Britain and the rest of Europe mixed with soft drinks such as tomato juice (Bloody Mary), ginger beer (Moscow Mule), or in cocktails. And remember, unlike other spirits, you should keep your vodka in the refrigerator, or at least chill it before serving.

Aquavit from Denmark and **Schnapps** from Germany are close relatives of vodka, being distilled from potatoes or grain. Aquavit is usually flavoured with anise, caraway or cardamom.

RUM

There's nought, no doubt,
so much the spirit calms
As rum and true religion

— LORD BYRON, *DON JUAN*

The Jamaicans will tell you that rum is a powerful medicine. They use it to treat cuts and bruises, to give relief from tooth and headaches, and even as a mild anaesthetic. But, anyone who has experienced Caribbean hospitality will tell you the sedative qualities are far from mild.

Rum is made from molasses — a thick, black and heavy syrup, the waste from the sugar refineries — which is diluted with water and mixed with yeast to ferment. Finally, this "wash" is distilled to create rum.

The rich brown hue of rum comes from caramel, which is used both as a colouring and a flavouring agent. Rum needs to be aged for several years before drinking.

It is believed rum got its name from *rumbullion*, a slang term for drunken rioting. There is a reference in the 17th century to a popular drink called "rumbullion, alias killdevil, and this is made of

RUM RUNNERS

sugarcanes distilled into a hot, hellish and terrible liquor".

ODD BUT TRUE: Perhaps the best "medicine" ever offered to a sailor was the brainchild of Admiral Vernon, who used it to combat scurvy among his Royal Navy sailors in the mid-18th century. In gratitude, they nicknamed him "Old Rummy".

However, by 1740, a stingy admiral named Edward Vernon decided that sailors should no longer receive their neat half-pint of rum daily, but that it should be diluted with water. His nickname was "Old Grog" because he wore a coat of grogram cloth — so the weaker drink became known as "grog". The daily grog ration was finally abolished on Royal navy ships in 1970

TEQUILA

It was cocktails like the *Margarita*, the *Brave Bull*, and the *Tequila Sunrise* which first made Mexico's fiery spirit popular in Britain and other Western nations. Made from the sap of the mezcal plant, tequila is double fermented in a copper pot still.

Mexicans traditionally drink tequila this way: Sprinkle a small amount of salt on the back of your hand, lick it, take a sip of ice-cold neat tequila, then suck a slice of lime.

LIQUEURS

Genghis Khan's favourite after-dinner drink was "lambwine", known in Chinese as *yan-yang-tskew*, and made from fermented lamb's meat or, in some provinces, from dogs.

Today's after-dinner drinks, or liqueurs, fortunately, are far more civilised. Known in the USA as "cordials", they are spirit based (and therefore quite potent) and are usually very sweet and aromatic.

Here are some of the main liqueurs a Drinking Man is likely to encounter:

AMARETTO Almond flavoured, made in Italy from apricot stones.

ANIS Tastes like licorice, from the aniseed used as flavouring.

BENEDICTINE Flavoured with 27 peels, herbs, and plants.

CHARTREUSE Flavoured with 130 herbs and spices.

CHÉRI SUISE Flavoured with cherries and chocolate.

COINTREAU Dry orange liqueur.

CREME DE CACAO Flavoured with cocoa beans and vanilla.

CREME DE CASSIS Flavoured with blackcurrants.

CREME DE MENTHE Peppermint; can be either green or white.

CREME DE NOISETTE Flavoured with hazelnuts; each bottle boasts a whole hazelnut.

CURACAO Flavoured with orange peel.

FRANGELICO Flavoured with hazelnut berries and herbs.

GALLIANO Flavoured with herbs, roots, and spices.

GRAND MARNIER Orange peel in Cognac.

IRISH MIST Flavoured with honey and herbs.

KAHLUA Flavoured with coffee.

KUMMEL Flavoured with caraway seeds.

MARASCHINO Flavoured with Dalmatian Marasca cherries.

MALIBU Jamaican rum Flavoured with coconut.

MIDORI Flavoured with Japanese melons.

OUZO Aniseed Flavoured liqueur from Greece.

SAMBUCA Licorice taste from elderbush flavouring.

TIA MARIA Flavoured with coffee and spices.

---

*I really like only champagne. The trouble is,
it gives you permanently bad breath.*

— ELIZABETH TAYLOR, QUOTED BY TRUMAN CAPOTE

**Beer is for women, wine for men
and rye for heroes.**

— OTTO VON BISMARCK

Drinker's I.Q. Test

No.7: ADVANCED CALCULUS

Add up the following:

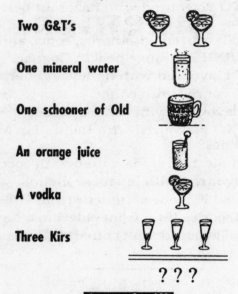

Two G&T's

One mineral water

One schooner of Old

An orange juice

A vodka

Three Kirs

? ? ?

Answers on Page 189

It was two o'clock in the morning when the phone started ringing. The publican reached over and answered. It was John, one of his regulars. "What time do you open in the morning?" came the slurred voice.

"Eleven o'clock!" replied the publican and slammed the phone down in disbelief.

Continued on Page 112 →

Drinking magpies

LOOKING for a genuine Drinking Man's hobby (apart from drinking, that is)? One that not only gives you a great deal of pleasure and a chance to meet regularly with other Drinking Men, but also gives you the best possible reason to surround yourself with lots and lots of drinks?

Well why not join the many people around the world who believe (and rightly so!) that everything about beer is precious so they collect a whole range of odds and ends relating to their favourite brew, from cans to labels and The study or collection of beermats is known as Tegestology. The term is derived from the Latin word for 'rug' or 'mat' which is 'Teges'.

Beermats originated on the continent and were made from pottery or porcelain. By 1892 the first wood-pulp beermats were being produced in Germany, but it wasn't until 1920 that the first such mat was made in Britain. That distinction fell to Watney's of London who produced two different mats advertising their Pale Ale and Reids Stout.

These early mats were a lot thicker than today's variety. Most of those produced before 1935 were up to a quarter of an inch or six millimetres thick. Nowadays they are more likely to be only an eighth of an inch or three millimetres.

Over the years many brains, both great and small, sober and drunk, have sought further uses for the humble beermat. The aerodynamics have been utilised to turn it into a spinning weapon.

Anybody caught short needing to write down an important phone number or make a quick calculation can also turn to the beermat. Tests of dexterity include building beermat versions of card-houses, and flipping piles of beermats into the air from the edge of a table and catching them. And if the table proves to be uneven, one may be inserted under one of the legs to correct the situation. even beermats.

When it comes to beer labels, there's no one to touch Norwegian Jan Solberg, whose collection totals more than 322,000! Austrian Leo Pisker, on the other hand, owns more than 130,000 beer mats from 153 countries.

The world's biggest collection of beer cans belongs to American John F. Ahrens of Mount Laurel, New Jersey, who has more than 15,000 tinnies from around the world. Australians, too, are fanatical beer can and bottle collectors, with the Downer Club in Canberra recently paying $25,000 for 2502 unopened bottles and cans from 103 countries at a charity auction.

Although a relatively new hobby, beer can collecting is catching on in many parts of the world.

One avid collector says his best haul ever was made

'HE'LL BE LIKE THAT UNTIL HE GETS ENOUGH CORKS FOR HIS NEW HAT...'

on the site of a demolished country pub. The new pub had been built across the road and all the old one's "rubbish" had been left behind. Of course, that rubbish was the collector's treasure — he walked away with four garbage bags full of old (and some very rare) cans, all in very good condition.

Condition, as in every other field of collecting, is of great importance in beer cans. Ideally, there should be no rust, no scratches on the paint, and the can should have been opened with two holes punched into the bottom, so that when it is displayed it appears to be full.

That's the way most beer can collectors drink their brew — from the bottom of the can!

Beer cans are best displayed in shelves about 2cm higher than the can. Collectors arrange them in many different ways: by country, subject, colour, patterns, to name only a few. And they certainly come in every colour imaginable and adorned with girls (including some great nudes), scenery, animals, rock and roll stars, hot-air balloons, sports stars, crests and even abstract designs. They also come in all sizes, from a mammoth one-gallon German drum to a US can holding a mere seven fluid ounces.

Of course, beer cans are not the only drink-related items that fascinate collectors. Here are some other world-beating collections:

☆ Ted Shuler of Germantown, Tennessee, claims to have the world's largest collection of different bottled beers — 2,248 specimens from 97 countries.

☆ *When it comes to beer labels, there's no one to touch Norwegian Jan Solberg, whose collection totals more than 322,000.*

☆ The world's biggest collection of beer mats is owned by Austrian fanatic Leo Pisker of Vienna, who boasts more than 130,600 different mats from 153 countries.

☆ *It took Briton David L. Maund more than 30 years to put together the world's best collection of different miniature Guinness bottles — all 323 of them. He also has close to 9000 unduplicated miniature Scotch bottles.*

☆ Edward Giaccone has 3100 unduplicated full-size whiskey bottles at his home in Lake Garda, Italy.

☆ *The world's largest collection of miniature distilled spirit and liquor bottles belongs to an American, George E. Terren, with more than 29,500 on display.*

Amazing facts about wine

... the vine, from whence we have that
nectarian, delicious, precious, heavenly,
joyful, and deific liquor...

— FRANÇOIS RABELAIS

 WINE is considered by many to be the nectar of the gods. It is made in great quantity and excellent quality in France, Italy, Germany, Australia, New Zealand, South Africa, and many other countries.

In fact, wine is probably the most talked about and written about beverage in the world. There are thousands of books about wine published every year, as well as a multitude of wine columns in newspapers and magazines. There are also many wine clubs and their newsletters which are packed with information about wine and vintages.

If you want to know about those aspects of wine, your best bet is to consult one of those specialist sources. In this chapter, we concentrate on the odd and amazing and gee-whizz aspects of wine that will fascinate your fellow Drinking Men as you casually recount them at a suitable moment in the pub or over dinner.

Talk about a calamity! Dried out by the heat from exhibition lights, in 1986 the cork on the world's most expensive bottle of wine slipped sufficiently to allow air to enter the bottle — and make the wine undrinkable!

Bought for 105,000 pounds sterling (around $220,000) by a wealthy American at Christie's in London only the previous year, the bottle of 1787 Chateau Lafite claret was engraved with the initials of Thomas Jefferson, third President of the United States. This added greatly to its value for collectors.

In June 1987 another bottle bearing the initials of Thomas Jefferson — this time a 1784 Chateau Margaux wine — fetched almost $40,000 at auction, the highest ever price for a half-bottle of wine.

How old is wine? The Bible tells us than Noah planted vines and made wine soon after the Flood (and got blotto soon after that), but now archeologists say many a tasty tipple had been enjoyed much earlier than that. They have found chemical evidence that around 3500 BC people were already quaffing good wine of a "robust vintage".

An earthen jar from Sumerian ruins recently excavated at Godin Tepe in western Iran was found to contain red-colored deposits rich in tartaric acid — and almost certainly the remains of an ancient wine, because tartaric acid is found in nature almost

Negotiating a WINEFIELD

exclusively in grapes.

According to Dr. Solomon H. Katz, an anthropologist at the University of Pennsylvania who specialises in early beverages, major cultural changes in that period were so stressful for locals that they turned to wine to forget their troubles.

"Almost from the start, wine has been a status symbol," says Dr Katz, who has traced the origin of beer brewed from barley back as far as 10,000 years ago.

The world's largest wine bottle, holding the equivalent of 44 normal bottles of Chateau La Rose Marechale 1985, was auctioned in 1988 in Copenhagen.

The coronation of Richard II in the 14th century saw probably more merriment than for any other English king — and not surprisingly, since the King treated his

London subjects by making fountains in the capital spout wine for hours.

His later namesake, Richard II, used wine in a different way — he had his brother Clarence drowned in a butt of malmsy in the Tower of London.

Drinking ten litres of wine a day, it would take a Drinking Man *more than 500 years* to empty the largest wooden wine cask in the world. The Heidelberg Tun, completed in 1751, is in the cellar of the Friedrichsbau, in Heidelberg, Germany and holds 1,855,000 litres.

The largest wine store today is at Paarl, South Africa, where 136 million litres are stored in a 10ha area.

Any storm in a PoRT.

Port was the favourite tipple of the victor of Waterloo, the Duke of Wellington. Port is red wine fortified with alcohol and takes its name from Oporto in Portugal where it originated.

Imagine paying almost $1000 for a *single glass* of wine! That's what French wine buff Bernard Repolt forked out for the first glass of Beaujolais Nouveau 1989. He said it tasted "heavenly".

The world's largest wine tasting, on the other hand, was staged by the Wine Institute in San Francisco on 17 July 1980. More than 125 people were needed to pour the 3000 bottles of wine that were drunk.

In Shakespearean times, vermouth was known as "wormwood wine". Vermouth is wine flavoured with, among other things, the flowers of the wormwood plant.

Madeira is a fortified dessert wine from the Atlantic Ocean island of the same name. And what higher praise can any drink receive than this one from the famous American author Nathaniel Hawthorne, in *The House of the Seven Gables*:

"The delicacies of the season, flavoured by a brand of old Madeira which has been the pride of many seasons. It is the Juno brand; a glorious wine, fragrant, and full of gentle might; a bottled-up happiness, put by for use; a golden liquid, worth more than liquid gold; so rare and admirable, that veteran wine-bibbers count it among their epochs to have tasted it! It drives away the heart-ache, and substitutes no head-ache! It would all but revive a dead man!"

Here's to champagne, the drink divine
That makes us forget our troubles;
It's made of a dollar's worth of wine
And three dollar's worth of bubbles.

☆ It was a Benedictine monk named Don Pérignon who is credited with discovering champagne. The years was 1668 and the young monk had been put in charge of his Abbey's cellar. One day, he accidentally got some carbonic gas into his wine

mixture — which he discovered when one of the bottles exploded. He investigated other bottles and found they were full of strange bubbles. He nervously took a sip of this sparkling wine and exclaimed: "I am drinking stars!" Champagne was born.

☆ A complete set of champagne bottles consists of a quarter bottle, a half bottle, bottle, magnum (2 bottles), Jeroboam (4 bottles), Rehoboam (6 bottles), Methuselah (8 bottles), Salmanazar (12 bottles), Balthazar (16 bottles), and finally the Nebuchadnezzar, which holds 20 bottles.

☆ The world's oldest champagne firm is Ruinart Pere et Fils founded in 1729.

Drinker's  I.Q. Test

No. 8: AT THE BAR

Flight AF 1037 was on a flight over some of the densest jungle in Africa. There were 38 passengers on board and four crew members of mixed nationality.

At precisely 12:05 pm they ran into some turbulence. Despite the best efforts of the pilot, the plane crashed. Only fifteen of the passengers and none of the crew survived the impact.

The plane's disappearance was noticed on the radar and a large search party was mobilised. After only two days the wreckage was located.

However, they discovered that the plane had crashed exactly on the border between the two countries. This prompted a political row.

Should the survivors be buried in the country from which the plane had taken off, or in the country to which it was heading?

Answers on Page 189

Fifteen minutes later the phone rang again.
"What time did you say you opened?" spluttered John.
"I said 11 o'clock, and I'm not going to let you in any earlier,"
replied the publican.
"I don't care about that," said John. "I only want to know
when I can get out of here!"

The wrath of grapes

Do not look at wine when it is red, when it
sparkles in the cup and goes down smoothly.
At the last it bites like a serpent and stings
like an adder.

— **PROVERBS XXIII, 29-32.**

 THERE'S nothing that afflicts a Drinking Man as much and as often as a Hangover. In the Drinking Man's guide to suffering, also known as *The Hangover Handbook and Boozer's Bible*, it is described aptly as a combination of Vesuvius erupting in your stomach, a bass drummer thumping on your brain, and a canary fouling its nest in your mouth.

Hangovers have not changed over the years. In Charles Dickens' classic *David Copperfield*, the young hero remembers "somebody, lying in my bed, at cross purposes, in a feverish dream all night — the bed a rocking sea, that was never still! How, as that somebody slowly settled down into myself, did I begin to parch, and feel as if my outer covering of skin were a hard board; my tongue the bottom of an empty kettle, furred with long service, and burning over a slow fire; the palms of my hands, hot plates of metal which no ice could cool!"

A hangover is caused by a combination of dehydration, too much fluid in the brain, too much lactic acid in the stomach, to much carbon dioxide in the blood, and a chemical created by alcohol which produces the most nauseating side effects.

How do you avoid a hangover?

Wowsers will say: Don't Drink! That's nonsense, of course — as is the idea that you can drink a lot and not suffer. Pleasure has to be paid for, and drinking is no exception. But there is a way you can at least minimise the suffering, by following this simple rule of thumb:

THE DARKER THE DRINK,
THE WORSE THE HANGOVER.

White drinks, such as still white wine, gin and vodka, are the safest. Vodka, in particular, is little more than alcohol and water and has no residual flavouring elements to be processed by your digestive system.

Sparkling drinks such as champagne, no matter how white, are dangerous. They contain more hangover causing acids (and also make you drunk more quickly).

Port, sherry, bourbon, rum and brandy are real killers. Malt scotch, strangely, has more impurities called congeners that cause hangovers than does blended Scotch, which among the dark drinks has the

I'LL BE GLAD WHEN I GET RID
OF THIS HANGOVER!

lowest hangover rating.

Although beer has the same low amount of congeners as vodka, you have to consume much more beer to get the same kick as from vodka, so you imbibe much more impurities than if you had stuck to vodka. So a beer hangover, on a drunkenness index, is quite severe.

Is there a cure for a hangover?

Film actress Tallulah Bankhead, renowned as a tippler in her day, remarked: "Don't be swindled into believing there's any cure for a hangover. I've tried them all: iced tomatoes, hot clam juiced, brandy punches. Like the common cold it defies solution. Time alone can stay it..."

However, over the ages Drinking Men have sought desperately for the elixir that will prevent or at least alleviate that dreadful suffering. If you want to know all about hangovers, your best bet is to invest in a copy of my specialist guide to the problem, *The Hangover Handbook and Boozer's Bible*. It contains over 100 recipes for the Drinking Man's malady — and a load of laughs as well.

But, in case you are in desperate need of instant treatment, here are some suggestions:

In parts of South America, every bar keeps a hangover cure known as *tratamiento de choque*. It smells awful but is said to work miracles and is made by soaking raw fish in onions, lemon juice and the sauce of hot peppers for two days. The sufferer breakfasts on this, together with popcorn for bulk and beer to wash it down.

English poet Lord Byron's Cure:
> *Let us have wine and women, mirth and laughter*
> *Sermons and soda-water the day after ...*

A prairie oyster is regarded by many as the ultimate cure for when you feel like death warmed up. It consists of a raw egg seasoned with salt, pepper and Worcestershire sauce, which is gulped down without swallowing.

In Japan, hangover sufferers walk around wearing a surgical mask — soaked in saki!

The hair of the dog that bit you has been a cure since Roman days — it means simply to have a drink or three for breakfast. It is in line with Dean Martin's advice: "Stay drunk!"

Other popular drink-based cures are:

☆ Bloody Mary: vodka and tomato juice.

☆ Black velvet: Guinness and champagne, half and half.

☆ A few cold beers.

Drinker's I.Q. Test

No. 9: (I)NTELLIGENCE (Q)UOTE

Match the following quotations with the famous people who
are alleged to have slurred them...

1.   I'm only a beer teetotaller, not a champagne teetotaller.

2.   Beer! O Hodgson, Guiness, Allsopp, Bass! Names that
      should be on every infant's tongue!

3.   I am falser than vows made in wine.

4.   Freedom and Whisky gang thegither!

A.   William Shakespeare

B.   Robert Burns

C.   George Bernard Shaw

D.   C.S. Calverley

Answers on Page 189

---

*"Don't have anything to eat on the way home after the
amount of grog you've put away tonight,"* the barman
warned Peter as he staggered to the door.
"Why not?" asked Peter.
*"It will make you feel sick in the morning and give you one
hell of a hangover!"*

Truly amazing!

HARRY Houdini was defeated only once in his famous escape routine from a padlocked submerged trunk — by beer. This happened in 1911 when British brewer Tetley's challenged him to escape from the trunk while the chest was submerged in beer, instead of the usual water. But the fumes were too much for the famous escapologist, who had to be hauled half-conscious from the tank.

Special bottles of saki, fermented to strains of Mozart's music, were sold in 1991 in Japan to commemorate the 200th anniversary of the famous composer's death.

Odd names for wine in English, although quite acceptable in their original language, include these cited by Robert Joseph in *The Wine Lists*:

France: *Les Blotters; La Clape; Les Pis; Les Migraines*
Germany: *Boos; Lump; Bunken*
Turkey: *Buzbag*
Italy: *Squinzano*
Algeria: *Mascara*

If you drank too much tequila in the days of the Aztecs, your condition was rated by other Drinking Men in terms of rabbits! One rabbit meant you were just starting; 10 rabbits indicated you were getting jolly, while 400 rabbits was the time you were ready to pass out.

When your time comes, what drinking man would not prefer to drown in a sea of beer? Actually, that happened to nine people way back in 1814 in the London parish of St Giles, when a brewery vat containing 3500 barrels of best beer burst — and flooded the neighbourhood. The river of beer swept through the crowded slum area, levelling at least two crumbling houses in its path, while smashing furniture, pets and people into one another.

When finally the flood stopped, the locals discovered that every single cellar in the parish had been filled with beer — a supply that kept everyone smiling for days.

Here's an infallible test to see if your host has poured you a good cognac (and not a cheap one decanted into an expensive brand's empty bottle):

Slosh the cognac around the glass so that it thoroughly wets the inside, then empty it (preferably into your mouth). Hide the glass and sniff it five or six hours later. If the aroma is still there, you've been drinking quality cognac.

A beer shop in north London has more than 500 beers in stock, including some of the rarest in the world. They include the following brands:

Old Fart

Willy Warmer

Baz's Bonce Blower

Son of a Bitch

Ever heard of the human champagne bottle? If you're a fan of mystery writer Edgar Allan Poe, you'll remember this description in the short story The System of Dr Tarr and Prof. Fether, where a lunatic "very rudely, as I thought, put his right thumb to his left cheek, withdrew it with a sound resembling the popping of a cork, and the, by dextrous movement of the tongue upon the teeth, created a sharp hissing and fizzing, which lasted for several minutes, in imitation of the frothing of Champagne".

If you thought the Pilgrim Fathers were a bunch of pious wowsers, you'll be surprised to discover they loved their beer so much they landed the Mayflower at Plymouth Rock in America ahead of schedule. As one noted in his diary: "For we could not take time for further search and consideration, our victuals being much spent, especially our beere." Soon after their arrival, another Pilgrim made it clear that they were so thirsty they would drink any kind of "beere":

If barley be wanting to make into malt,
We must be content and think it no fault,
For we can make liquor to sweeten out lips,
Of pumpkins, and parsnips, and walnut
tree chips.

The charming Rhineland town of Alzey is not only a great place to sample some of the world's best wines. A visit to its museum brings you face to face with the remains of the oldest known German beer — a hard brown-black mass unearthed near the town and dating from the fourth century AD.

Cider was so much more popular for drinking than water in some parts of England that the Anglican Church once had to decree sternly that infants were not to be baptised in it.

Imagine sweating off your hangover this way! In the Middle Ages, many villages in Europe used not only the stocks in which to punish Drinking Men who overstepped the limit, but some used a special barrel to hold the offender, with holes for his arms and legs. This was called a "drunkard's coat", shown above.

The patron saints of publicans is the fourth-century St Martin of Tours.

Bavaria boasts the world's oldest still-operating brewery, founded in 1040 at Freising.

At least one American president was elected because of cider. During the 1840 election, William Henry

Harrison dispensed the golden liquor in liberal quantities to anyone who qualified as a voter — and in return a great many voted for such a generous man.

What on earth do you think is the occupation of a *Koeniglichbayrischeroberbiersteuerhaupteinkassierer*? In Germany before the First World War, when this was the official title of the collector of taxes on beer in Bavaria. The 51-letter word translates to "royal Bavarian superior beer-tax chief cashier".

Why is it quite fit and proper to get drunk in Manhattan? Because the name (from the Indian word for the New York island, *Manahachtanienk*) literally means "the place where we all got drunk". It was so named after Indians enjoyed a drink or twenty at a party given by Captain Henry Hudson after he sailed into New York Bay in 1609 on board his ship *Half Moon*.

Ancient Egyptian doctors believed fervently in the value of beer to treat every kind of disease (including, of course, the occasional hangover). Archeologists have found over 100 recorded medicines containing beer as the basic fluid.

An enterprising Israeli company produces Kosher vodka.

Iceland's national drink is a kind of aquavit they call *brannvin* — which translates to *Black Death*. But at least

it's unlikely to be as potent as Chinese snake wine, the essential ingredient of which is a full-size snake marinated inside the bottle for up to 20 years.

Kvass is a Russian beer made from fermented rye bread.

Even today rum cannot be made legally in England. Instead, new Jamaica spirits are shipped to London and then aged in wooden casks in bonded warehouses on the London dockside. They are known as *London Dock* rums when bottled — and taste quite different to rum aged in the West Indies.

Danzig Goldwasser (literally *Danzig's golden water*) is an exotic liqueur flavoured with caraway and aniseed and decorated with *real* flakes of gold suspended in the liquid.

The golden-brown Linie Aquavit matures in a most amazing way — by taking a round trip from Norway to Australia while it ages in wooden casks stored in the holds of ships bound for Australia!

According to well-known wine writer Rosalind Cooper in her book *Spirits and Liqueurs*, "the warm voyage lets the spirit mature rapidly and gives it a smooth taste. Upon return to Norway, the aquavit is bottled. Each label indicates the ship that carried the aquavit across the Equator."

Here's an unusual way for Drinking Men to play a game and get drunk at the same time — if you're any good, that is.

The idea comes from Graham Greene's well-known novel *Our Man in Havana*, where two characters play a game of draughts using, as pieces, 12 miniatures of Scotch for one side and 12 miniatures of bourbon for the other. You get to drink every piece you capture!

But be careful — in the Greene novel, the winner passes out.

While on the subject of miniatures: the smallest liquor bottles on sale are for White Horse Scotch Whisky. They contain 1.3 ml of whisky and stand just over 5 cm high. You can also buy them by the 12-bottle case.

How to sip and save

EVERY Drinking Man likes to drink a lot — without spending a fortune. The only problem is that cheap booze tastes horrible — and gives you a hangover you'll never forget!

But there is a way to drink and drink and drink top quality booze — and still have a pocket full of cash.

The secret is home-made beer, wine and liqueurs. And before you pull a face and say, "The only home brew I ever had was undrinkable", think again. Today's sophisticated beer, wine and liqueur making kits make brewing as easy as quaffing a few cans — it only takes a little longer.

There has been a great resurgence of home brewing in the last few years. This is mainly attributable to the excellent quality and huge range of brew concentrate "can kits" now available, which work well with improved brewing equipment.

"Today, by using readily available sealed

fermenting vessels it is possible to maintain a perfect sterile environment for yeasts, and by so doing make a pure natural beer which can be better tasting than the majority of commercial beers," says John Wilson, an expert in the home brew arena and author of the authoritative *How To Brew Your Own Beer Manual*.

Below are John's tips for making perfect beer of all varieties at home — and *for about a quarter of the cost of commercial beer*.

Home brewing is no longer limited to basic beers only. You can home brew excellent German all-malt lager types, strong English barley wines, non-alcoholic natural ginger beers and lemonades for wives and wowsers, and even full strength (40° proof) liqueurs can be home brewed.

Low cost

Yet the costs involved in starting your home brewery are very low. The average cost of a "starter" fermenter/equipment kit, which contains the ingredients for 30 big bottles of beer is around $60. Buying that amount of commercial beer will cost you about the same — yet by investing in a brewing kit you go on making beer at a quarter of the cost you paid before. Thus, even from the outset, your home brewing starting equipment is free!

Great quality

Home brewed beer has traditionally suffered from a reputation of having a nasty "home brew" taste, and there is truth in this. However, this taste comes from two sources which a good brewer can easily eliminate.

The first taste is chlorine, which is present in tap water. This can be driven off the water by boiling all the water needed the day before brewing. Alternatively, pass the water through an **activated carbon** water filter.

The second taste is induced by using cane sugar in the fermentation. Cane sugar fermentation leaves a "cidery/acid" flavour in home brew not found in commercial beer. Using "brewers sugar", known technically as dextrose (a form of glucose), eliminates this undesirable flavour and acidy aroma. Dextrose has no flavour and thus allows the true taste of the malt and hops to dominate.

There are three levels of complexity in home brewing.

Concentrate can brewing. This is the choice for you if all you want is cheap beer even if it is not as good as commercial beer. This usually involves using one make of concentrate can bought at the local supermarket and using unfiltered tap water and cane sugar.

Malt brewing. Here you can use concentrate cans as a starting base, but by adding such ingredients as pure malt extract, hops, dextrose, and filtered water, you can produce beer as good as the best from boutique breweries and expensive European imports. You can also brew sugar-free (all-malt and hops only) German-style beer with or without small quantities of added malted grains for distinctive flavour balancing.

Malt extract brewing is probably the fastest growing segment of home brewing, as the quality and beer styles are almost limitless. In fact, world-renowned home-brewer Charlie Papazian estimates there are 20,000 types of beer possible from home brewing.

Mash brewing. This is brewing the way it was done for generations before the advent of the concentrate cans and good malt extract was available. Still the purest form of brewing, it involves "mashing" (controlled temperature soaking) of the malted grains (usually barley) to remove the soluble sugars necessary for the yeast fermentation. This is followed by boiling the resulting sweet liquid with hops to achieve particular flavour balance and style, before fermenting to create pure beer. It takes about half a day to put down a mash brew.

To start your home brewing, buy your starter/fermenter kit from a home brew specialty shop because it is important that you first brew is a success. Experienced advice will help you achieve that.

Although starter kits have instructions included, many of the instructions are not that clear, so it is important to have someone you can turn to for advice. Your home brew specialist retailer is usually a keen brewer who will be only too willing to help you get started — and make sure you succeed.

Better still, John Wilson's excellent *How To Brew Your Own Beer Manual* covers every step from "getting started", through to "malt brewing", plus general information to help you make every brew a winner. Very soon you could be brewing your own ale at a microbrewery and selling it to an appreciative pub or two!

You can also make your own wines (from fruit, vegetables, even grass-clippings) and liqueurs. There are also an increasing number of excellent home kits available for this. However, it is a specialised area and you should consult your local home brew shop or an experienced Drinking Man before starting.

The Drinking Man's Dictionary

AMERICANS

*Most Americans are born drunk... They have
a sort of permanent intoxication from
within, a sort of invisible champagne...
Americans do not need to drink to inspire
them to do anything.*

— G.K. CHESTERTON

BALANCED DIET

A drink in each hand.

— ANONYMOUS

CHARACTER

*Something tested through business, wine,
and conversation.*

— ANONYMOUS

COCKTAIL PARTY

An excuse to drink for those who don't need excuses.

A cocktail is to a glass of wine as rape is to love.

— PAUL CLAUDEL

CONVERSATION

The enemy of good wine and food.

— ALFRED HITCHCOCK

DEATH

The first drop kilt me; the last was harmless.

— SEUMAS MACMANUS

DIPLOMACY

Protocol, alcohol, and Geritol.

— ADLAI STEVENSON

DOCTORS

There are more old drunkards than old doctors.

— BENJAMIN FRANKLIN

DRINKING

First the man takes a drink, then the drink takes a drink, and finally the drink takes the man.

— ANONYMOUS

Something to do while getting drunk.

— PEGGY BRACKEN

Putting an enemy in your stomach to steal away your brains.

— ANONYMOUS

DRUNKARD

Like a whiskey bottle, all neck and belly and no head.

— AUSTIN O'MALLEY

One who can live neither with alcohol nor without it.

— ANONYMOUS

He is a drunkard who takes more than three glasses, though he be not drunk.

— EPICTETUS

(One who can) always beer up under misfortune.

— MARCELENE COX

ELOQUENCE

What one thinks he has after a cocktail.

— WARREN GOLDBERG

ENEMAS

He drinks beer, a habit no more
bacchanalian than taking enemas.

— MAXWELL BODENHEIM

ENGLISHMEN

*They are like their own beer: froth on top,
dregs on the bottom, the middle excellent.*

— VOLTAIRE

INTOXICATION

To feel sophisticated and not be able to
pronounce it.

— ANTHONY B. LAKE

MADNESS

*Drunkenness is nothing else than a
voluntary madness.*

— SENECA

MUSIC

The brandy of the damned.

— GEORGE BERNARD SHAW

PROHIBITION

Although man is already ninety per cent water, the Prohibitionists are not yet satisfied.

— JOHN KENDRICK BANGS

SOBRIETY

There is nothing wrong with sobriety in moderation.

— JOHN CIARDI

SOPHISTICATION

The art of getting drunk with the right people.

— LEONARD L. LEVINSON

TEETOTALLER

I am only a beer teetotaller, not a champagne teetotaller.

— GEORGE BERNARD SHAW

THINKING

When I drink, I think; when I think, I drink.

— FRANÇOIS RABELAIS

TIME

These are long times between the drinks!

— G.B. BURGIN

WILLINGNESS

I am willing to taste any drink once.

— JAMES BRANCH CABELL

WINE

Wine is bottled poetry.

— ROBERT LOUIS STEVENSON

WISE

Those who drink old wine and see old plays.

— PLAUTUS

WOMEN

Women will be as pleasing to men as
whiskey when they learn to improve as
much with age.

— FRANKLIN DANE

Happiness is... your own bar!

WHEN it comes to entertaining at home, there's nothing to beat your own bar. Of course, you'll ensure it's stocked with plenty of that Drinking Man's staple diet — booze. But to entertain your guests in the style befitting friends of a true Drinking Man, you'll also need the following equipment for your bar:

Double-ended measuring cup

Lime-squeezer

Mixing spoon

Professional bar shaker with a wire strainer for cocktails

570ml glass beaker with pouring lip

Cutting board to prepare fruit for drinks

Sharp fruit knife

Ice bucket and ice crusher

Electric blender

If your budget permits, a small bar fridge.

In addition to a range of mixers, you'll need at least the following spirits:

Scotch whisky	Bourbon
Brandy	Coffee liqueur
Cointreau	Creme de Cacao
Galliano	Gin
Grenadine	Rum (white and dark)
Tequila	Vermouth (dry
Vodka	and sweet)

The art of mixing cocktails

A little whiskey to make it strong,
A little water to make it weak,
A little lemon to make it sour,
A little sugar to make it sweet.

— ANONYMOUS

Generally, *cocktails* is accepted today as a generic term for all mixed drinks. Special glasses are not really necessary — almost any container, from a coconut shell to a pineapple, can be used to hold a cocktail attractively. As a guideline, however, choose stemmed glasses for cocktails which are not served on ice, as they will stay cooler longer, and tumblers or highball glasses for drinks which require ice. Short cocktails look their best in traditional triangular cocktail glasses, while goblet styles are generally used for drinks incorporating egg yolks.

All cocktails are served cold. It makes a great

difference if the glasses have been chilled. Ideally the glasses should stand in the refrigerator for an hour or two before needed, but a scoop of ice placed in the glass and left there while the drink is being prepared will chill it very effectively.

Cocktails have a language all their own: when someone asks for one "straight up", it means served without ice. Other terms you're likely to encounter are:

✔ *On the rocks* — with ice

✔ *Strain* — pour mix through strainer to remove ice chips and fruit

✔ *Twist* — a small strip of lemon peel, sharply twisted to bruise the rind; this allows oil to escape into the drink when the peel is floated.

All cocktails must be measured carefully and as long

'THE LONE RANGER! YOU'LL FIND HIM DOWN THE STREET IN THE SINGLES BAR...'

as the measure remains constant throughout the recipe, the drink will have the correct flavour and consistency. Cocktails are made four ways:

Shaking

This method is usual for sweet-and-sour, sweet and cream-type drinks. You can use either cracked or cubed ice. Pour the ingredients into a cocktail shaker, add a handful of ice, shake briskly and serve as soon as the outside of the shaker begins to sweat.

Stirring

This is for martini-type drinks where you want to make sure the base spirit is not bruised. Pour the ingredients into a 570ml glass beaker with a pouring lip, then stir with a clean bar spoon. Use ice blocks, not chips, and serve immediately before the ice dilutes the mixture.

Floating

This is done when a recipe calls for a cream or high-proof spirit to be floated on top of the mixed ingredients. Take a bar spoon (or a curved dessert spoon), hold it upside-down so the bottom touches the side of the glass, just above the other ingredients, then carefully pour the spirit or cream over it.

Blending

If your recipe calls for fresh fruit or eggs, they will need to be blended to give them a frothy consistency. Pour the ingredients together with ice into an electric blender, then blend briefly. Never put a carbonated ingredient into your shaker, mixing glass or liquidiser. By the same token, glasses should not be filled to the brim — and remember to leave room for your garnish.

Cocktails should be served fresh as they will separate if left too long. Always hold the glass by the stem or the base to avoid fingerprints and unnecessary warming of the drink.

Garnishes

A garnish should enhance a drink without disguising it. It can be anything from a floating flower to a stuffed green olive speared on a cocktail stick.

Slices of lemon, orange and lime are the most frequently used garnishes, along with cocktail cherries. Spear the garnish on a coloured swizzle stick.

With tropical fruit drinks garnish with fruits such as pineapple, mango and kiwifruit.

Savoury garnishes include pearl onions, cucumber slices and stuffed olives together with sprigs of fresh mint. Celery salt and paprika are sometimes sprinkled over the finished drink before serving.

An attractive way to enhance a sweet cocktail is to dip the rim of the glass in sugar. Sour drinks may be dipped in salt crystals.

The tale behind the cocktail...

Some experts say the first recipe for a cocktail was a concoction of lemon juice and powdered adders, which was praised highly by the Emperor Commodus in the second century AD as an aperitif!

So where does the word cocktail come from? There are many stories, some more plausible than others. One traces it to an Aztec overlord in Mexico whose beautiful daughter was called X-octl. Some American officers went to visit her father and, after a pleasant meeting, were served some exotic mixed drinks. The officers said they would never forget X-octl, so they decided to name the drinks after her. The closest they could come to pronouncing her name was "cocktail" — and a legend was born.

Another story says that during the American War of Independence, an innkeeper named Betsy Flanagan, whose premises were frequented by Lafayette's as well as Washington's officers, once prepared a meal of chickens she stole from a pro-British neighbour. To celebrate this small victory she decorated glasses used at the feast with feathers plucked from the chickens.

"I'M NOT DISCRIMINATING, IT'S JUST I DON'T BELIEVE YOU'RE EIGHTEEN!"

Her French clients heartily toasted her with cries of *Vive le cocktail!*

There are numerous other possibilities for the origination of the term cocktail, but perhaps one of the most likely involves the tails of horses. Non-thoroughbreds, those of mixed stock, would have their tales docked. These became known as 'cock-tailed' horses. Therefore any drink, not of pure spirit, also became known as a cocktail.

☆ The first true book of cocktails was by Jerry Thomas, who published in 1862 *The Bon Vivant's Guide or How to Mix Drinks.*

☆ The largest cocktail on record is a *Pina Colada* of 1486.6 litres, mixed in Germany in August 1988 by Kai Wulf, Ivano Birello and Axel Bornemann.

"I ONLY CAME IN FOR A BAG OF SMOKEY BACON CRISPS !!"

Mixing it in style!

HERE'S your chance to mix drinks of every colour and flavour imaginable — and have a ball sampling every one! Armed with the list below, you should be able to meet virtually every request for a cocktail.

A quick note before you start mixing (and drinking): if you worry about nothing else, try to get the proportions of the different ingredients right. When "part" is used in the recipes below, it refers to the standard "jigger" holding 45ml. If you want to use a different measure, go ahead — so long as you use the ingredients in the same proportion as shown in the recipe. Also, recipes are usually per person, so increase the measures by the number of people you are providing for.

Glass sizes:

Collins 300-420ml   Highball 240-300ml
Whisky tumbler 180-250ml
Sour 120-180ml   Cocktail 120ml

' YOU'RE RIGHT, IT ISN'T TRADITIONAL
— BUT IT'S A LOT BETTER THAN A
ST BERNARD LICKING YOU TO DEATH !'

GIN

Astoria

1 dash orange bitters
2 parts gin
1 part dry vermouth

Shake ingredients well with ice and strain into a cocktail glass

Caruso

1½ parts gin
1 part dry vermouth
1 part green crème de menthe

Shake ingredients well with ice or stir in a mixing glass with ice. Strain into cocktail glass.

Gibson

2½ parts gin
½ part dry vermouth
2 cocktail onions

Stir gently in mixing glass with ice. Strain into cocktail glass. Add onions. Garnish with lemon peel.

Gin and tonic

2 parts gin
Lime wedge
Tonic water

Pour into highball glass with ice. Stir well.
Garnish with lemon wedge.

Gin Fizz

2½ parts gin
1 part lemon juice
1 teaspoon castor sugar
4 parts club soda

Combine gin, sugar, lemon juice in shaker
with ice cubes. Shake well. Strain into glass
almost filled with ice cubes. Add club soda. Stir
well.

Gin Sour

2 parts gin
½ teaspoon castor sugar
1 part lemon juice
1 maraschino cherry
1 slice orange

Combine gin, sugar, lemon juice in shaker
with ice cubes. Shake well. Strain into glass.
Garnish with cherry and orange slice.

Marguerite

2 parts gin
1 part dry vermouth
1 dash orange bitters
1 twist orange peel
1 maraschino cherry

Stir well in mixing glass with ice. Strain into glass. Garnish with orange peel and cherry.

Martini

1 part gin
1 part dry vermouth

Shake ingredients well with ice and strain into a cocktail glass. Decorate with a twist of lemon peel or a stuffed olive.

Martini Sweet

2 parts gin
1 part sweet vermouth

Shake the ingredients well with ice and strain into a cocktail glass.

Martini Dry

Four part Tanqueray gin
One part dry vermouth

Stir gin and vermouth with ice. Strain into chilled cocktail glass. Garnish with lemon twist.

"TO BE HONEST, SVEN THE LADS THINK YOU'VE LOST YOUR BOTTLE!"

Gimlet

1 part gin
1 part lime cordial

Stir gin and lime cordial together. Serve in a cocktail glass; if preferred partly filled with crushed ice.

Gin Sour

8 parts gin
1 part lime or lemon juice
1 part sugar syrup

Shake well with ice and strain into a glass.

Pink Gin

2 parts gin
Dash Angostura bitters
1 ice cube

Swirl bitters inside cocktail glass. Add gin, ice. Dilute with water, soda water or tonic.

Red Lion

1 part gin
1 part Grand Marnier
Juice of ¼ lemon and ¼ orange

Shake. Strain into cocktail glass.

Singapore Sling

Created at the famous Raffles Hotel in Singapore in 1915

Two parts gin

One part cherry brandy

One part orange juice

Soda water

Dash bitters

Shake ingredients well with ice cubes. Pour into highball glass. Top up with soda. Decorate with pineapple wedge and maraschino cherry.

Tom Collins

2 measures gin

Juice of ½ lemon

1½ teaspoons caster sugar

soda water

Shake the ingredients with ice and strain into a tall tumbler. Add ice, use soda water to top up. Decorate with cocktail cherries and lemon slices.

White Lady

Two parts gin

Two parts cream

One part Crème de Cacao

Blend with crushed ice. Strain into a small martini glass.

VODKA

Bloody Mary

1 part vodka
2 parts tomato juice
1/3 part lemon juice
Dash of Worcestershire sauce
Salt and pepper

Shake well with ice. Strain into wine glass.
Garnish with celery leaves or a slice of pepper.

Black Russian

2 parts vodka
1 part Kahlua

Pour over ice cubes into whisky tumbler.

Black eye

2 parts vodka
2/3 part blackberry juice

Mix with ice. Strain into old-fashioned glass
almost filled with ice. Stir well.

Chi Chi

Three parts vodka
Two parts coconut cream
Eight parts pineapple juice
Two scoops crushed ice

Blend all ingredients together with the ice. Garnish with a slice of fresh pineapple and a cherry.

Harvey Wallbanger

2 parts vodka
²⁄₃ part Galliano
3 parts orange juice

Stir orange juice and vodka in highball glass with ice. Float Galliano on top.

Moscow Mule

1 part vodka
3 parts ginger beer
²⁄₃ part lemon juice
1 lime wedge

Stir vodka, ginger beer, lemon juice in highball glass with ice cubes. Garnish with lime wedge.

"LET'S FACE IT, DARLING. CREIGHTON'S, NOT AS YOUNG AS HE USED TO BE — WE'RE GOING TO HAVE TO GET A SHORTER TABLE!"

Russian cocktail

1 part vodka

½ part gin

½ part white crème de cacao

Stir vodka, gin, white crème de cacao with ice.
Strain into cocktail glass.

Screwdriver

Four parts orange juice
One part vodka

Pour vodka and orange juice over ice. Serve.

Vodka Collins

2 parts vodka
Juice of 1 lime
1 teaspoon caster sugar
Soda water

Shake well with ice. Strain into collins glass
with ice. Top up with soda water. Garnish with
cherry and lime and lemon slices.

Vodka Dry

1 part vodka
1 teaspoon dry sherry
1 lemon twist

Swirl sherry in whisky tumbler to wet inside.
Pour out remainder. Stir vodka into mixing
glass with ice. Strain into tumbler. Garnish
with lemon twist.

Vodka martini

1 part vodka
1 part dry vermouth

Shake well with ice. Strain into cocktail glass.
Garnish with lemon twist.

White Russian

2 parts vodka
1 part Kahlua
Thickened cream

Pour over ice cubes into whisky tumbler. Pour cream over back of a spoon to form a thick layer on top.

RUM

Bacardi Cocktail

1 part Bacardi light rum
1 part lime juice
1 teaspoon grenadine

Shake well with ice. Strain into cocktail glass.

Boston Sidecar

1 part light rum
½ part Cointreau
½ part lemon juice

Shake well with ice. Strain into cocktail glass.

Cuba Libre

2 parts dark rum
Juice of ½ lime
Cola

Pour rum, lime juice into collins glass. Add cola. Stir. Garnish with lime slices.

Daiquiri

2 parts rum (light or dark)
Juice of ¼ lemon
1 teaspoon caster sugar

Shake well with ice. Strain into cocktail glass. Garnish with cocktail cherry.

Grog

2 parts light rum
3 parts water

Pour into old-fashioned glass. Stir well.

Nevada

Two parts under-proof rum
One part lime juice
Two parts grapefruit juice
One part sugar syrup

Shake together all ingredients.

Pina Colada

---

2 parts dark rum
2 tablespoons crushed pineapple
3 tablespoons coconut milk

Blend with two cups of ice in electric blender till smooth. Stain into collins glass. Serve with straw.

Planters Punch

---

1 part dark rum
1 part light rum
1 part anejo rum
1 part lime juice
½ part lemon juice
3 parts club soda
1 orange slice
1 lime wedge
1 pineapple wedge
1 maraschino cherry
2 teaspoons caster sugar

Shake rum, lime and lemon juice, sugar well with ice. Strain into collins glass part-filled with ice. Top up with soda water. Garnish with fruit.

Sorry... no ice

Rum Cocktail

1 part light rum
1 teaspoon grenadine
2 teaspoons fresh lime or lemon juice
half teaspoon sugar

Blend or shake together very well. Serve straight up in a cocktail glass or on the rocks.

Rum Collins

2 parts dark rum
1 teaspoon caster sugar
Juice of 1 lime
Soda water

Shake well with ice. Strain into collins glass with ice. Top up with soda water. Garnish with cocktail cherry and lemon slice. Serve with straw.

Rum Crusta

1½ parts dark rum
½ part Cointreau
½ part lemon juice
2 teaspoons maraschino liqueur
1 tablespoon caster sugar
1 lemon wedge
Spiral-cut peel of 1 orange
Crushed ice

Place sugar in saucer. Rub lemon wedge over rim of a wine goblet. Dip glass into sugar to thickly coat rim. Place orange peel spiral in wine goblet with one end draped over rim of the glass. Fill the glass with crushed ice. Shake maraschino liqueur, Cointreau and rum with ice. Strain into wine goblet.

Smiling Ivy

One part under-proof rum
One part peach liqueur
One part pineapple juice
Dash lemon
Egg white

Shake together all ingredients.

ANOTHER?

maybe just a SHORT one

Tiny Tim

1 part white rum
1 part dry vermouth
1 part pineapple juice
Dash of grenadine

Stir with cracked ice.

Zombie

1 part light rum
1 part dark rum
1 part pineapple juice
1 teaspoon caster sugar

Shake well with ice. Strain into collins glass. Garnish with pineapple slices and cocktail cherry.

BRANDY

Brandy Alexander

1 part brandy
½ part crème de cacao
1 part thickened cream
Grated nutmeg

Shake with ice and strain into wide champagne glass. Sprinkle lightly with grated nugmeg.

Brandy Fix

1 part brandy
½ part cherry brandy
1 teaspoon caster sugar
1 teaspoon water
Juice of ½ lemon
1 lemon slice

In a tumbler, dissolve the sugar in water. Add ingredients. Fill with crushed ice. Stir. Garnish with lemon slice. Serve with straw.

Brandy Flip

2 measures brandy

1 dash bitters **½ teaspoon curacao**

½ teaspoon sugar

Shake well. Strain into tumbler. Garnish with
lemon peel and 1 sprig mint

Corpse Reviver

1 part brandy

½ part sweet vermouth

½ part Calvados

Shake well with ice. Strain into cocktail glass.

Sidecar

1 part brandy

½ part Cointreau

½ part lemon juice

Shake well with ice. Strain into cocktail glass.

Stinger

¾ *part brandy*
¼ *part crème de menthe*
Shake well with ice. Strain into cocktail glass.

TEQUILA

Corcovado

1 part tequila
1 part Drambuie
1 part blue Curaçao
Lemonade
1 lemon slice

Shake ingredients well with ice. Strain into
collins glass filled with crushed ice. Top up
with lemonade. Garnish with lemon slice.
Serve with a straw.

Margarita

1 part tequila
1 dash Triple Sec
Juice of half a lime

Pour over crushed ice and stir. Rub the rind of
the lemon on the rim of a stem glass, spin the
rim in salt. Pour the drink into the glass and
sip through the salt.

Mexicana

2 parts tequila
1 part pineapple juice
½ part lemon juice
1 teaspoon grenadine

Shake ingredients well with ice. Strain into cocktail glass.

Tequila Moonrise

3 parts tequila
1 part dark rum
1 part light rum
2 parts beer
½ part lemon juice
1½ parts Rose's lime juice
1 teaspoon caster sugar.

Shake all ingredients (except beer) well with ice. Strain into collins glass with ice. Top up with beer.

Tequila Sunrise

1½ parts tequila
½ parts grenadine
3 parts orange juice
1 orange slice
2 cocktail cherries

Shake tequila and orange juice with ice. Strain into collins glass. Float about 4 ice cubes on top. Slowly add grenadine, allow it to settle. Garnish with orange slice and cherries.

Viva Vegas

1 part tequila

½ part lime juice

½ teaspoon grenadine

¼ part maraschino

½ egg white

Shake ingredients well with ice. Strain into wide champagne glass filled with crushed ice. Garnish with cocktail cherry, slices of lime and lemon.

WHISKIES & BOURBON

Bobby Burns

1 part Scotch
1 part sweet vermouth
3 dashes Benedictine
Lemon peel

Shake well with ice. Strain into cocktail glass. Garnish with lemon peel.

"FORGET IT — SHE'D MELT YOUR IGLOO!"

Dixie Stinger

---

3 parts bourbon

½ teaspoon Southern Comfort

½ part white crème de menthe

Shake well with ice. Strain into cocktail glass.

John Collins

---

2 parts bourbon

1 part lemon juice

3 parts club soda

1 teaspoon caster sugar

1 orange slice

1 maraschino cherry

Shake all ingredients except club soda with ice. Strain into collins glass with ice. Top up with club soda. Stir. Garnish with cherry and orange slice.

Manhattan

---

2 parts Canadian whisky

1 part sweet vermouth

1 dash Angostura bitters

Shake well with ice. Strain into cocktail glass.

Manhattan Dry

1 part Canadian whisky
½ part dry vermouth
½ part sweet vermouth

Stir with ice, Strain into cocktail glass.

Mint Julep

3 parts bourbon
1 teaspoon caster sugar
6 fresh mint sprigs, stems cut short

Dissolve sugar with a few drops of water in highball glass. Fill glass to near top with crushed ice. Add bourbon. Garnish with mint on top. Serve with short straws.

Old-Fashioned

2 parts Canadian whisky
2 dashes Angostura bitters
1 lump of sugar
1 orange slice
Twist of lemon peel

Soak sugar with bitters in whisky tumbler, Crush sugar with the back of a spoon. Add ice, orange slice, lemon twist. Add whisky. Stir well.

Rusty Nail

1 part Scotch
1 part Drambuie

Pour Scotch onto ice in whisky tumbler. Pour Drambuie over back of a spoon so it floats on top of Scotch.

Whisky Sour

2 parts whisky
1½ teaspoons sugar
Juice of ½ lemon
Soda water
1 orange slice
Cocktail cherry

Shake well with ice. Strain into whisky tumbler. Add soda water to taste. Garnish with cocktail cherry and orange slice.

AMAZING CONCOCTIONS

Egg Ale was a somewhat remarkable — and, on the face of it, a slightly revolting — concoction, although said to be highly nutritious. The old recipe stipulated:

To twelve gallons of ale was added the gravy of eight pounds of beef. Twelve eggs, the gravy beef, a pound of raisins, oranges and spice, were then placed in a linen bag and left in the barrel until the ale had ceased fermenting. Even then an addition was made in the shape of two

quarts of Malaga sack. After three weeks in cask the ale was bottled, a little sugar being added. A monstrously potent liquor truly!

To make *Rumfustian*, a popular drink last century, mixing a quarter bottle of rum, the same of, a large bottle of beer, a bottle of sherry, 12 egg yolks, sugar, nutmeg, spices, and orange peel. Drink it and prepare for spontaneous combustion!

Flip, a very popular drink for our ancestors, is made this way, according to an old recipe:

Place in a saucepan one quart of strong ale together with lumps of sugar which have been well rubbed over the rind of a lemon, and a small piece of cinnamon. Take the mixture off the fire when boiling and add one glass of cold ale. Have ready in a jug the yolks of six or eight eggs well beaten up with powdered sugar and grated nutmeg. Pour the hot ale from the saucepan on to the eggs, stirring them while so doing. Have another jug at hand and pour the mixture as swiftly as possible from one vessel to the other until a white froth appears, when the flip is ready. One or two wine glasses of gin or rum are often added.

☆ **Depth Charge** — Budweiser with a shot of bourbon.
☆ **Dog's Nose** — Redback beer with a shot of gin.
☆ **Submarino** — San Miguel with a shot of tequila.

Eat, drink and be merry!

"Fry six rashers of fat bacon
When done add one pint of good rum
Eat the bacon and drink the syrup.

 DAREDEVIL frontiersman and dedicated Drinking Man Colonel William Byrd jotted down that recipe for his favourite breakfast way back in 1728. It's a great, albeit rather extreme, example of the way drink and food enhance one another.

Wine snobs spend their lives arguing about which wine goes best with what type of food. The experienced Drinking Man knows you can (and should) always drink what you enjoy most — no matter what you are eating. In most cases, your own well-developed drinking taste will guide you unerringly to pick the most appropriate drinks for the occasion.

However, to make this survival guide complete, here's a quick summary of the conventional wisdom about what drinks best enhance which foods.

Wine

- ✔ Canapes, crackers, olives, cheese dips and other hors d'oeuvres: sherry, vermouth, or champagne.
- ✔ Soups: sherry or Madeira.
- ✔ Seafood: Chablis, Rhine wine, Moselle, dry sauterne, white Burgundy.
- ✔ Poultry and game birds: Rhine wine, dry sauterne, champagne, Bordeaux, white or red Burgundy.
- ✔ Red meats: claret, red Burgundy, rose.
- ✔ Cheese or nuts: port, sherry, red Burgundy, muscatel.
- ✔ Desserts: sweet sauterne, champagne, port, muscatel, Tokay.
- ✔ After dinner: brandy, Cointreau, benedictine, creme de menthe.

Beer

One of the great recent developments has been the acceptance of beer the British Drinking Man's nectar as a great drink at the dinner table. As the range of available beers have increased, so beer lists HAVE started becoming much more common in hotels and restaurants.

Beer is a great accompaniment for almost every kind of food, as our ancestors knew only too well.

In many parts of Europe, particular the cold northern regions, people for centuries began and ended their days with beer. As Michael Weiner points out in *The Taster's Guide to Beer*, the day began with "a good draught to wet your whistle; at the noonday meal a beer soup; and at supper, of course, there must be egg-flip made with beer. Raisin beer and sugar beer, fish and sausages boiled in beer, beer in all conceivable forms, to say nothing of abundant draughts of plain beer when paying visits, talking business, attending baptisms and funerals..."

England, too, had a great tradition of serving beer with food. The following charges appear in the household expenses of King Henry VIII:

The queen's maids of honour to have a chet loaf, a manchet, a gallon of ale, and a chine of beef for their breakfast. The brewer is informed not to put any hops or brimstone in the ale.

Today, lovers of barbecues and Asian foods know the golden brew enhances the taste of meat and spicy dishes.

But beer can compliment most other dishes as well. Just pick the correct brew and you can serve — and enjoy — beer with every course (except dessert, unless you are a real beer lover, that is!).

☆ For pre-dinner drinks, offer your guests light, bitter, cold beer which will excite the gastric juices and work up an appetite.

☆ Guinness goes down great with **oysters** served with brown bread, butter and lemon and with **shellfish** of every description.

☆ For **main courses**, serve a strong, full-bodied beer (not too cold) with meat dishes and casseroles. Curries also call for a full-bodied strong brew, but much colder. With spicy Oriental food, a sweetish, light to medium beer is the ideal companion.

Eating your beer

Of course, if you're a true beer lover, you'll also want to cook with beer. The Vikings of old loved their beer so much they included a soup made of their favourite brew with every meal — and they ate six times a day!

In fact, the Drinking Men of the past seemed to appreciate the many culinary uses of beer far more than we do today.

Last century beer mixed with brown sugar was a favourite sauce for pancakes; red herrings were steeped in small [weak] beer before being broiled; and catsup (the forerunner of today's ketchup) for sea stores was made mainly of beer and vinegar.

Here are a few beer recipes to get you tasting beer food:

Melon cocktail

Cut a large honeydew melon in half. Remove pips and scoop out balls. Place in a shallow dish and pour in beer until the melon balls are just covered. Stand for about 15 minutes, then put melon balls in cocktail glasses and cover them with chilled beer. Serves 6.

Beer Soup

Beer soup (*bier suppe*) was a regular part of the diet of 17th century Prussian schoolboys.

600ml beer

600ml milk

2 egg yolks, beaten

1 teaspoon butter

half teaspoon salt

1 dessertspoon honey

Mix milk and beer, simmer for 15 minutes; add salt and honey; remove from heat and stir in butter and beaten egg yolks.

Beer Steak

500g rump steak

350ml beer

2 large onions

2 tablespoons butter

Salt and black pepper

Melt butter in shallow saucepan, add peeled and sliced onions and fry slowly until brown. Season steak, then place in saucepan on top of the onions. Cover and simmer on low heat for 90 minutes. Pour in the beer and continue simmering for two-and-a-half hours. Remove steak, thicken gravy with flour. Serve with mashed potatoes and vegetables.

Seafood-'n-beer casserole

250g prawns, cooked and shelled
250g tinned crab meat
4 cups beer
24 oysters
2 onions
4 shallots
1 stick of sliced celery
1 teaspoon parsley
50g butter
1 tablespoon flour
salt and pepper to taste

In shallow saucepan, bring to boil the beer, onions, parsley, celery and shallots. Simmer for 15 minutes. Season with salt and pepper. Add prawns, oysters and crab meat. Mix flour and butter into a paste, then add to the saucepan and stir until boiling. Serve with rice.

Beer bread

1 cup beer
250g plain flour
1 cup wholemeal flour
2 tablespoons caster sugar
15g yeast

Take a loaf tin 20x10x8cm and grease. Cream the yeast and sugar in a warmed basin until liquid. Bring beer to boil, then allow to cool until tepid. Stir the beer into the yeast, then add butter and continue stirring with wooden spoon to a smooth dough. Brush with melted butter, then cover and leave in warm place until the dough doubles in size. Punch down. Cover, wait until it doubles in size again. Punch down again, then shape into the tin and cover the top with melted butter. Leave in warm place until double in size, then bake in moderate oven (190°C., 375°F. for about one hour or until ready.

Ale and apple pie

600ml hot spiced ale
4 large cooking apples
2-3 tablespoons sugar
Grated peel of half lemon
Short pastry

Wash and core apples, then place them next to one another in a large pie dish. Mix butter, sugar and lemon peel into a firm paste. Pack into the cored hollows and smear surplus paste over the apple tops. Cover the dish with short pastry. Bake in hot oven (250°C., 450°F.) until pasty has risen. Lower to moderate (125°C.,350°F.) and bake until pastry is brown. Carefully remove pastry without breaking. Pour the hot spiced ale over the apples, cut the pastry into four and cover each apple with pastry. Serve with fresh cream.

I SEE THE COUNTESS IS STILL HAVING A SECRET AFFAIR WITH THAT, LAUTREC, FELLOW ...

Here's to your birthday!

EVERY Drinking Man loves a party — and what better excuse than to celebrate a birthday! The problem is, you'll almost certainly run out of family and friends who have birthdays when you are thirsty. So, as part of your survival guide, here are 366 famous (and a few infamous) people you can toast with a drink or three on their birthdays.

There are all kinds of ways you can celebrate these birthdays. You can do so with other Drinking Men, or on your own. You can celebrate all day, or only after work. It's entirely up to you.

Celebrating American Independence day, for instance, you could start with a lunchtime drink similar to that enjoyed daily by George Washington. According to a friend, the founder of modern America dined "at three ... and drinks half a pint to a pint of Madeira wine. This with one small glass of punch, a daught of beer, and two dishes of tea". The friend went on to describe Washington as "very regular, temperate and industrious"!

JANUARY

1	J. Edgar Hoover	16	Singer Ethel Merman
2	Isaac Asimov	17	Mohammed Ali
3	Author J.R.R. Tolkien	18	Comic actor Oliver Hardy
4	Jane Wyman	19	Dolly Parton
5	King Juan Carlos of Spain	20	Slim Whitman
6	Joan of Arc	21	Benny Hills
7	"Addam's Family" creator	22	Beatrice Potter
	Charles Addams	23	Humphrey Bogart
8	Elvis Presley	24	Neil Diamond
9	Martin Luther King	25	Robert Burn
10	Rod Stewart	26	Australia
11	Rod Taylor	27	Mozart
12	Joe Frazier	28	Alan Alda
13	Sir Joh Bjelke-Petersen	29	W.C. Field
14	Faye Dunnaway	30	Gene Hackman
15	Aristotle Onassis	31	Mario Lanza

FEBRUARY

1	Clark Gable	16	John McEnroe
2	Farah Fawcett	17	Banjo Patter
3	Val Doonican	18	Yoko Ono Lennon
4	Alice Cooper	19	Lee Marvin
5	Reggae performer Bob Marley	20	Sydney Poitier
6	Ronald Reagan	21	Russian Czar Peter III
7	Charles Dicken	22	Washington
8	James Dean	23	Handel
9	Mia Farrow	24	Alain Prost
10	Robert Wagner	25	Renoir
11	Thomas Edison	26	Victor Hugo
12	Abraham Lincoln	27	Elizabeth Taylor
13	Kim Novak	28	Boxer Barry McGuigan
14	Every love	29	Indian leader R.M. Desai
15	Jane Seymour		

MARCH

1	David Niven	17	Every Irishman
2	Singer Karen Carpenter	18	Rimsky-Korsakov
3	Alexander Graham Bell	19	Wyatt Earp
4	Vivaldi	20	Dame Vera Lynn
5	Singer Elaine Page	21	Bach
6	Dame Kiri Te Kanawa	22	Karl Malden
7	Viv Richard	23	Joan Crawford
8	Lynn Redgrave	24	Steve McQueen
9	Mickey Spillane	25	Elton John
10	Prince Edward	26	Diana Ross
11	Rupert Murdoch	27	Michael York
12	Liza Minnelli	28	Dirk Bogarde
13	Joe Bugner	29	Journalist Chapman Pincher
14	Albert Einstein		
15	Attila the Hun	30	Rolf Harris
16	Matthew Flinders	31	Haydn

"THIS WILL BE A LONG, BORING SPEECH — HE'LL DO ANYTHING TO GET OUT OF THE WASHING UP!!"

APRIL

1	April Fool	16	Spike Milligan
2	Cassanova	17	James Last
3	Doris Day	18	Einstein
4	Elmar Bernstein	19	Dudley Moore
5	Bette Davis and	20	Ryan O'Neil
	Spencer Tracy	21	Queen Elizabeth
6	Houdini	22	Alan Bond
7	William Wordsworth	23	Shakespeare
8	Sonja Henie	24	Barbra Streisand
9	Hugh Heffner	25	Al Pacino
10	Omar Sharif	26	Koo Stark
11	Actress Jill Gascoine	27	Samuel Morse
12	Maria Callas	28	Ann-Margret
13	Thomas Jefferson	29	Emperor Hirohito
14	Rod Steiger	30	Pop star
15	Samantha Fox		Bobby Vee

MAY

1	Glenn Ford	17	"Sugar" Ray Leonard
2	Author Jerome K. Jerome	18	Perry Como
3	Engelbert Humperdink	19	Nellie Melba
4	Audrey Hepburn	20	James Stewart
5	Karl Marx	21	Fats Waller
6	Robert Browning	22	Footballer George Best
8	Sonny Liston	23	Joan Collins
9	Barbara Woodhouse	24	Queen Victoria
10	Pop star Donovan	25	Marshal Tito
11	Salvador Dali	26	Queen Mary
12	Florence Nightingale	27	Wild Bill Hickok
13	Joe Louis	28	Patrick White
14	Bobby Darin	29	Bob Hope
15	James Mason	30	Benny Goodman
16	Henry Fonda	31	Clint Eastwood

GOSH! POWDERED RHINO HORN SOUFFLE AND CHAMPAGNE FOR SUPPER — ARE YOU TRYING TO GIVE ME INDIGESTION, MR HUMBLETON ?!

JUNE

1	Superman	16	Actor Stan Laurel
2	Johnny Weissmuller	17	Barry Manilow
3	Tony Curtis	18	Garfield
4	King George III	19	Duchess of Windsor
5	Singer Bill Hayes	20	Errol Flynn
6	Bjorn Borg	21	Jean-Paul Sartre
7	Pop star Tom Jones	22	Meryl Streep
8	Nancy Sinatra	23	Sir Leonard Hutton
9	Cole Porter	24	Lord Kitchener
10	Judy Garland	25	George Orwell
11	Jacques Yves Cousteau	26	Colonel Tom Parker
12	Author Charles Kingsley	27	France's King Louis XII
13	Poet W.B. Yeats	28	Mel Brook
14	Burl Ive	29	Nelson Eddy
15	Actress Nicola Pagett	30	Mike Tyson

JULY

1	Princess Diana	17	Donald Sutherland
2	Betty Grable	18	John Glenn
3	Richard Hadlee	19	Ile Nastase
4	The USA	20	Sir Edmund Hillary
5	P.T. Barnum	21	Swaziland's King Sobhuza II
6	Sylvester Stallone	22	Terence Stamp
7	Pinnochio	23	Emperor Haile Selassie
8	John D. Rockefeller	24	Amelia Earhart
9	Barbara Cartland	25	First test-tube baby
10	Marcel Proust		Louise Brown
11	Yul Brynner	26	Mick Jagger
12	Henry Thoreau	27	Allan Border
13	Harrison Ford	28	Sir Garfield Sober
14	Ingmar Bergman	29	Mussolini
15	Linda Rondstadt	30	Henry Ford
16	Explorer Amundsen	31	Evonne Goolagong

AUGUST

1	Yves St Laurent	17	Mae West
2	Peter O'Toole	18	Robert Redford
3	Martin Sheen	19	Orville Wright
4	Percy Bysshe Shelley	20	John Emburey
5	Harold Holt	21	Princess Margaret
6	Robert Mitchum	22	Claude Debussy
7	Greg Chappell	23	Golfer Peter Thomson
8	Dustin Hoffman	24	Max Beerbohm
9	Rod Laver	25	Elvis Costello
10	Herbert Hoover	26	John Buchan
11	Alex Haley	27	Tarzan
12	Cecil B De Mille	28	Goethe
13	Alfred Hitchcock	29	Michael Jackson
14	Sarah Brightman	30	Frankenstein creator
15	Napoleon		Mary Shelley
16	Madonna	31	Mad Emperor Caligula

"WE'RE JOLLY LUCKY TO HAVE THE ENTERTAINMENTS OFFICER ON OUR RAFT ..."

SEPTEMBER

1	Engelbert Humperdick	16	Peter Falk
2	Russ Conway	17	Roddy McDowell
3	Alan Ladd	18	Gandhi
4	Dawn Fraser	19	Mickey Mouse
5	Racquel Welch	20	Sofia Loren
6	Lafayette	21	H.G. Wells
7	J. P. Morgan	22	Captain Mark Phillips
8	Harry Secombe and Peter Sellers	23	Bruce Springsteen
9	Cardinal Richelieu	24	Linda McCartney
10	Arnold Palmer	25	Ronnie Barker
11	Ferdinand Marcos	26	Ian Chappell
12	Maurice Chevalier	27	Pop star Alvin Stardust
13	Claudette Colbert	28	Brigitte Bardot
14	Actor Jack Hawkins	29	Jerry Lee Lewis
15	Agatha Christie	30	Deborah Kerr

OCTOBER

1	Walter Matthau	17	Evel Knievel
2	Groucho Marx	18	Chuck Berry
3	Chubby Checker	19	Adam Lindsay Gordon
4	Charlton Heston	20	Bela Lugosi
5	Bob Geldof	21	Alfred Nobel
6	Tony Greig	22	Joan Fontaine
7	Clive James	23	Diana Dors
8	Juan Peron	24	The Big Bopper
9	John Lennon	25	Helen Reddy
10	James Clavell	26	Mahalia Jackson
11	Bobby Charlton	27	John Cleese
12	Luciano Pavarotti	28	Hank Marvin
13	Margaret Thatcher	29	Joseph Goebbels
14	Cliff Richard	30	Henry "The Fonz" Winkler
15	John L. Sullivan		
16	Oscar Wilde	31	Eddie Charlton

NOVEMBER

1	Gary Player	16	Frank Bruno
2	Marie Antoinette	17	Sir Charles Mackerras
3	Charles Bronson	18	George Gallup
4	Loretta Swit	19	Jodie Foster
5	Lester Piggott	20	Robert Kennedy
6	Ray Coniff	21	Goldie Hawn
7	Marie Curie	22	Tom Conti
8	Alain Delon	23	Billy the Kid
9	Hedy Lamarr	24	Ian Botham
10	Richard Burton	25	Karl Friedrich Benz
11	Rodney Marsh	26	Tina Turner
12	Grace Kelly	27	Jimi Hendrix
13	Robert Louis Stevenson	28	Randy Newman
14	Prince Charles	29	Louise May Alcott
15	Mantovani	30	Winston Churchill

DECEMBER

1	Madame Tussaud	17	Kerry Packer
2	Painter George Seurat	18	Betty Grable
3	Joseph Conrad	19	Edith Piaf
4	Pamela Stephenson	20	Sir Robert Menzies
5	Walt Disney	21	Frank Zappa
6	Ira Gershwin	22	Dame Peggy Ashcroft
7	Eli Wallach	23	J. Arthur Rank
8	Sammy Davis Jr	24	Colin Cowdrey
9	Kirk Douglas	25	Sissy Spacek
10	Jahangir Khan	26	Richard Widmark
11	Singer Brenda Lee	27	Marlene Dietrich
12	Frank Sinatra	28	Actress Maggie Smith
13	Dick van Dyke		
14	Nostradamus	29	Mary Tyler Moore
15	Nero	30	Rudyard Kipling
16	Noel Coward	31	John Denver

DRINKER'S IQ TEST ANSWERS

Question 1 : Answer: D. This shows you are a discerning drinker, timing your run perfectly. If you selected (A) your crotch is ruling your head. If you selected (C), your stomach is ruling your head. And if you selected (B) there is not much in your head.

Question 2: Cognac = 6; Armanac = 6; Aquavit = 5; Bourbon = 8; Slivovitz = 3; Vodka = 15; Curacao = 2; Irish Whiskey = 4; Scotch = 11; Sake = 10; Schnapps = 14; Rum = 7; Tequila = 13; Calvados = 9; Arak = 7.

Question 3: Answer: No. If you can, you are either (1) Cheating by reading the answers at the same time, (2) a Pom, (3) so drunk you've passed gone into a horizontal position.

Question 4: Answer: C. That handle is one drop short of a full measure.

Question 5: One tonne of these crisps would work out to $24,000. Other prices roughly are (A) Aluminium $1666, (B) Copper $2100, (C) Potatoes $100, (D) Sugar $370, (E) Nickel $8800, (F) Gas Oil $260, (G) Live pigs $2200.

Question 6: If ... (A) Seek a cooler spot, (B) Seek the owner of the dog, (C) Seek directions to the dunny, (D) Seek medical attention.

Question 7: Either (1) A cheque book job, (2) A man on a hen night, (3) Time to duck your round.

Question 8: In neither country. You would not bury the survivors.

Question 9: 1 - C in "Candida" (1898), 2 - D in "Beer", 3 - "A in As You Like It", 4 - B in "The Author's Earnest Cry and Prayer".

Have you ever suffered from a

HANGOVER?

Have you ever groaned and burped and cursed the morning after as Vesuvius erupted in your stomach, a bass drummer thumped on your brain, and a canary fouled its nest in your throat?

Then we have a book for you!

THE HANGOVER HANDBOOK AND BOOZER'S BIBLE

It's so authentic it's even cut in the shape of a beercan

The book is not meant to remind you of those gruesome mornings, but to help you beat them in future with **more than 100 amazing - and often amusing — hangover remedies** from battle-scarred drinkers the world over. There's even an exclusive **Hangover Ratings Chart** so you - and not fate - can decide exactly how much you want to suffer tomorrow.

But that's not all!

There's a unique **Boozer's Calendar,** which gives you 365 reasons to have a drink - one for every day of the year.

You meet the **Great Drunks of History.** You find out what's on offer at the world's first **Hangover Clinic.**

And if anyone dares to claim you're drunk, you can easily prove them wrong with our exclusive **Boozer's Reading Chart.**

Win round after round of drinks by challenging your drinking buddies to the stimulating **Boozer's Quiz** (you can't lose because we give you the answers).

See Page 192 for details

MORE HUMOUR TITLES...

The Ancient Art of Farting by Dr. C.Huff
Ever since time began, man (not woman) has farted. Does this ability lie behind many of the so far unexplained mysteries of history? You Bet - because Dr. C.Huff's research shows conclusively there's something rotten about history taught in schools. If you do most of your reading on the throne, then this book is your ideal companion. Sit back and fart yourself silly as you split your sides laughing! *£3.99*

A Wunch of Bankers
Do you HATE BANKS? Then you need this collection of stories aimed directly at the crotch of your bank manager. A Wunch of Bankers mixes cartoons and jokes about banks with real-life horror stories of the bare-faced money-grabbing tactics of banks. If you think you've been treated badly, read these stories!!!! *£3.99*

Down the Pan: Amuse Yourself in the Toilet
Do you have fun in the toilet? Or, do you merely go about your business and then depart? Instead of staring at the floor and contemplating the Universe, you could be having a ball! Here is an hilarious collection of *cartoons, jokes* and *silly stories*... a gruesome description of *great toilet accidents*... Discover the *secret card tricks*... Europeans may turn straight to the Franglais conversation sur la bog... Look at famous toilets of history... Learn to juggle toilet rolls! . £3.99

The Bog Book
(In the shape of a toilet seat)
How much time do you spend in the bog every day? Are you letting valuable time go to waste? Not any longer! Now you can spend every second to your advantage. The Bog Book is packed with enough of the funny, the weird and the wonderful to drive you potty. Fill your brain while you empty your bowels! £3.99

The Armchair Guide to Football
An inexpensive and humorous look at the state of modern football. Is it really run by money crazed businessmen who don't care about tradition? Will Fantasy Football remove the need for pitches, players and footballs? Only £1.99

The Armchair Guide to Golf
From the serious handicap hunter to the weekend hacker, everybody involved with golf will appreciate this humorous view from the 'inside'. Only £1.99

MORE GOOD BOOKS...

Sex Trivia
Are you a sex addict? What about your partner? Well, here's a bedside
companion that is titillating, weird, exotic, bizarre, sizzling, shocking,
stupendous, hilarious, oddball, staggering... and packed with thousands of
TRUE FACTS (all you've ever wanted to know) about everyone's favourite
pastime! £3.99

The National Lottery Book: Winning Strategies
An indispensable guide to the hottest lottery systems in the world. All
designed to help you find those lucky lottery numbers that could make you
rich. ● Learn how to *Play Like the Pros*... ● Discover ways of *Getting an
Edge*... ● Improve your chances with the *'Wheeling Technique'*... ● Find
possible ways of *Making it Happen* for you... ● See how understanding betting
Psychology and Equitability can seriously *Improve Your Winnings*... ● Plus
lots more *General Tips* to help you win! £4.99

Rude Cats (for cat lovers everywhere)
If you have ever wondered what your average moggie has been up to as it
staggers back over the garden wall, covered in scar tissue and licking its
rear end, then "RUDE CATS" is for you. Join Randy, an old campaigner
on a sexually explicit journey of discovery into the twilight world beyond
the cat-flap and prepare to be shocked! £3.99

*If you would rather not damage
your copy of Drinking Man's
Survival Guide, please use plain
paper and remember to include all
the details listed below!*

Postage is FREE within the U.K. Please add
£1 per title in other
EEC countries and
£3 elsewhere.

VISA

Please send me a copy of
☐ I enclose a cheque/payment made payable to 'Take That Ltd'.
☐ Please debit my Access/Visa card number
Signature: _____ Expiry Date: _____

Name: _____
Address: _____
_____
_____ Postcode: _____
Please return to: **Take That Books, P.O.Box 200, Harrogate, HG1 4XB**